Mondrian
A–Z

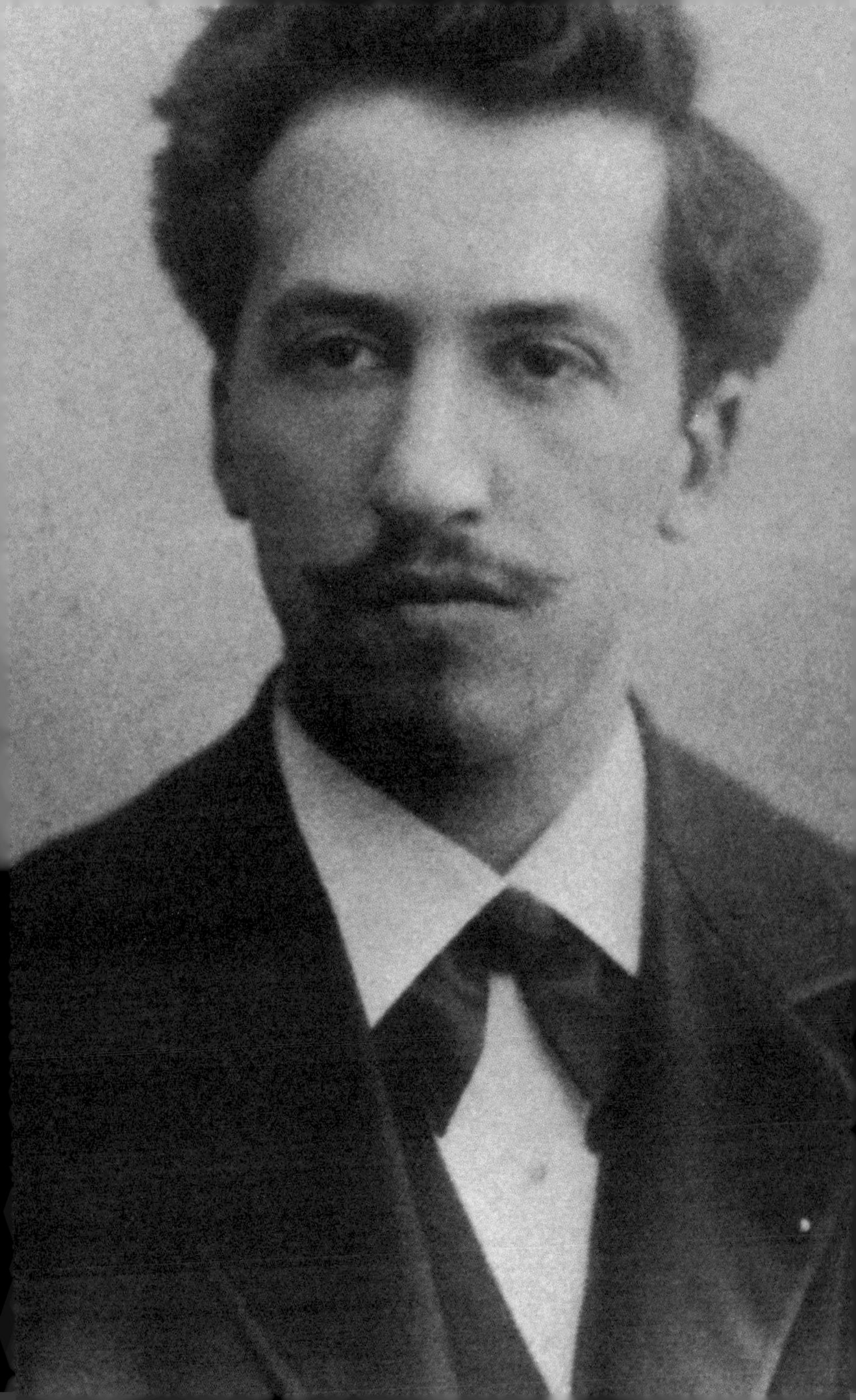

Piet Mondrian
A–Z

Ulf Küster

HATJE
CANTZ

Preface

Piet Mondrian was one of the most versatile artists of the modern era. He not only painted and drew, but also extensively reflected on and wrote about his sometimes complicated ideas and theories of art and life. Understandably, the literature on him has become almost insurmountable. This A to Z is an attempt to blaze a trail through the jungle of information on Mondrian. In as succinct a form as possible, with few notes, well-known and less well-known aspects of his life and work are presented above all for an interested general audience. The selection of terms is subjective and does not claim to give a complete account of Mondrian's life. It is, rather, about providing inspiration to reflect and to continue to work on this fascinating artist.

In 2022, it will be the 150th anniversary of Piet Mondrian's birth, and *Mondrian A–Z* is being published on that occasion. It also accompanies the exhibition *Mondrian Evolution*, which will be shown in 2022–23 at the Fondation Beyeler, Basel/Riehen, and at the Kunstsammlung Nordrhein-Westfalen, K20, Düsseldorf.

A → Abstraction
Abstract Paintings

On January 29, 1914, Piet Mondrian wrote a programmatic letter from Paris to his patron Hendricus Petrus ("HP") Bremmer. In it, he sketched his artistic impetus and his method. He sought to construct "on flat surface lines and colour combinations with the aim of, as deliberately as possible, depicting general beauty." Mondrian continued: "Nature (or that which I see) inspires me, gives me, just as it does any painter, the emotion, the prompts, the urge to make something, but I want to get as close as possible to the truth and am therefore abstracting everything until I get to the foundation (albeit still an outward foundation!) of things."[1]

Mondrian was describing abstraction as a process for approaching the absolute truth and beauty for which he was striving as an artist.

When he wrote this letter, he was working on a series of paintings that had been inspired by Cubism.→Cubism That process of abstraction was not yet completed in 1914.

Mondrian's development in the direction of what he felt was the truth led him in the years that followed to brief phases of representational painting,→Duivendrecht, →Windmill then to modular, regular color-field compositions, and finally around 1920 to the completely nonrepresentational, abstract paintings for which the artist is still world-famous today. Mondrian had found a way to get as close as possible to the "foundation . . . of things," even if it was only the "outward foundation."

A *Wall Structure of a Demolished House in Paris* 1913–1914
Pencil sketchbook 11, fol. 21 17.2 × 10.5 cm
Kunstmuseum Den Haag

Translating this drawing into an abstract painting:
Composition No. VI
[Composition No. VI / Compositie 9] (Blue Façade) 1914
Oil on canvas 95.2 × 68 cm
Fondation Beyeler, Beyeler Collection, Riehen/Basel

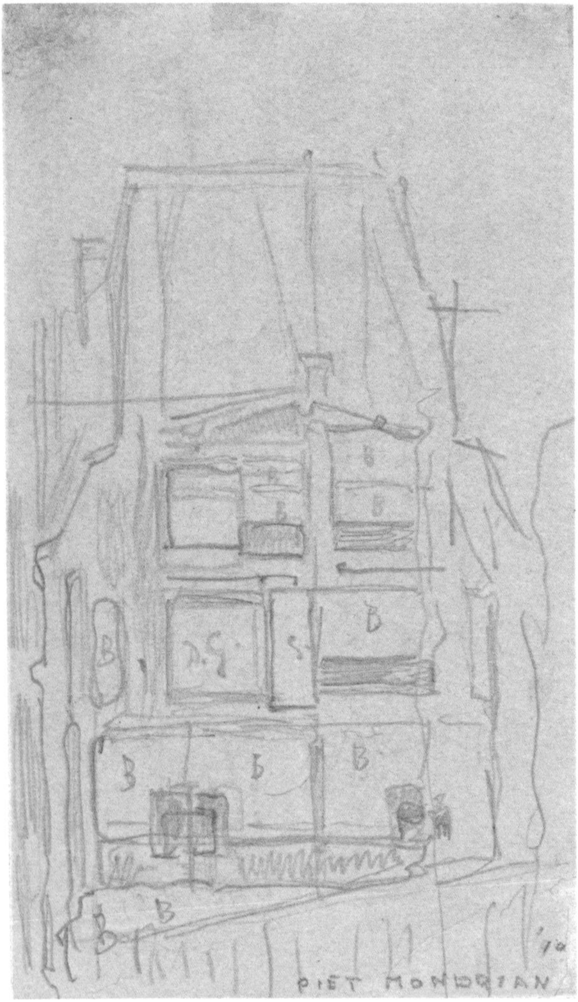

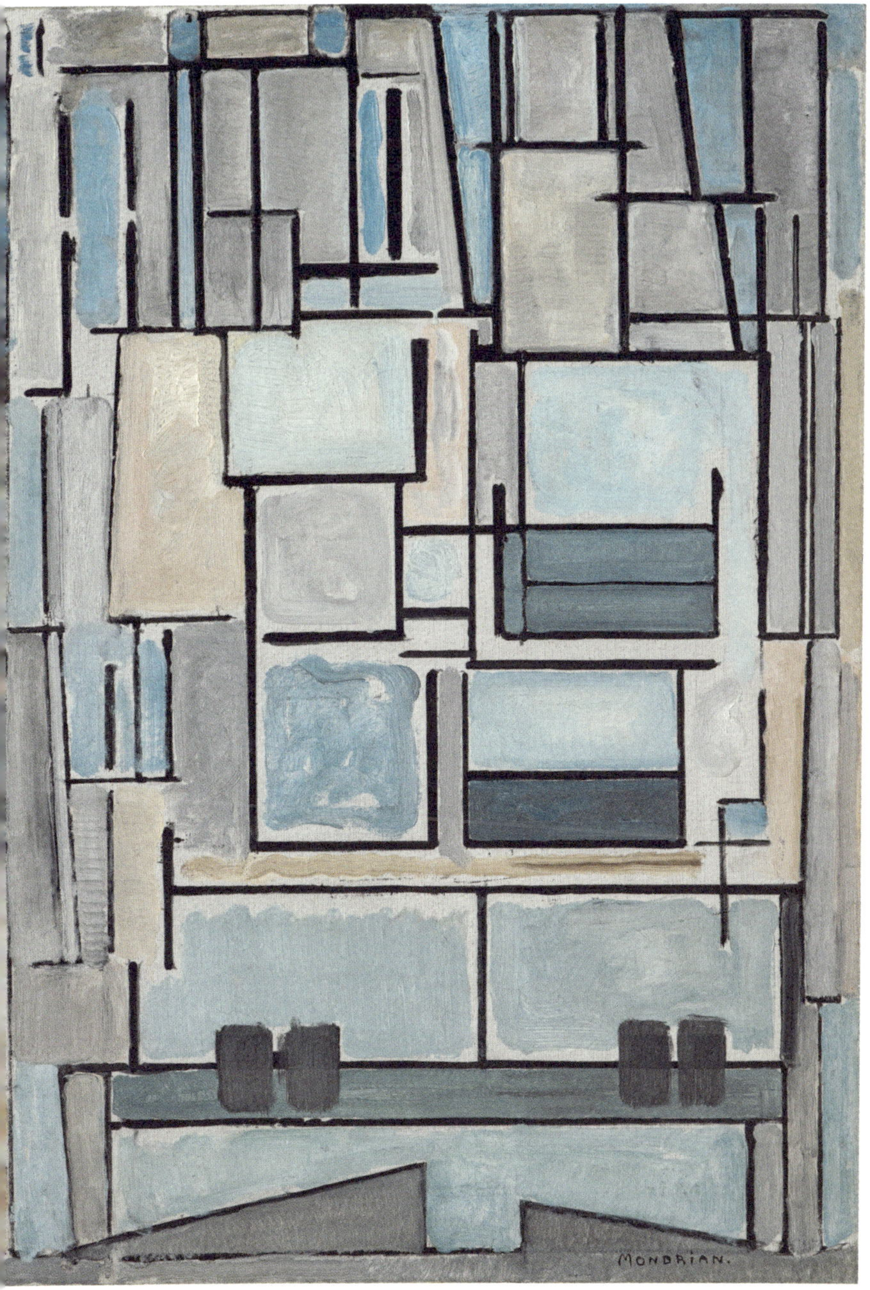
MONDRIAN.

B → Bacteria

It is a little-known fact that Mondrian worked as a scientific illustrator for Reinder Pieters van Calcar, who was a professor of bacteriology at the University of Leiden and made a name for himself as a cholera researcher.

The reason why it is so little known is that apparently no documents of Mondrian's work have been preserved. There are drawn illustrations in Calcar's publications, but when they are signed, it is not by Mondrian. He is, however, said to have worked for him since 1896 and was apparently still doing so as late as 1910. It is not known when he stopped. Mondrian, who for a time sold no paintings or only a few, was able to earn a little money in this way.

But earning money will not have been the only thing that interested Mondrian about scientific drawings of bacteria. It offered him an opportunity to penetrate to the core of life, which was also his motive to work as an artist. → Abstraction And he was able to observe that the microcosm is based on exact laws that find their correspondence in the macrocosm.

What he was able to practice when working for the University of Leiden was the precision of craft → Precision and Intuition that will later have helped him draw exact black lines in nonrepresentational paintings. It is said that he did not use a ruler to do so. Perhaps his drawings of flowers—above all, chrysanthemums—which as are empathetic as they are precise, best convey a sense of what his renderings of bacteria might have looked like.

B *Chrysanthemum in a Bottle* ca. 1906–08
Watercolor and pencil on paper 28.3 × 21.3 cm
Private collection

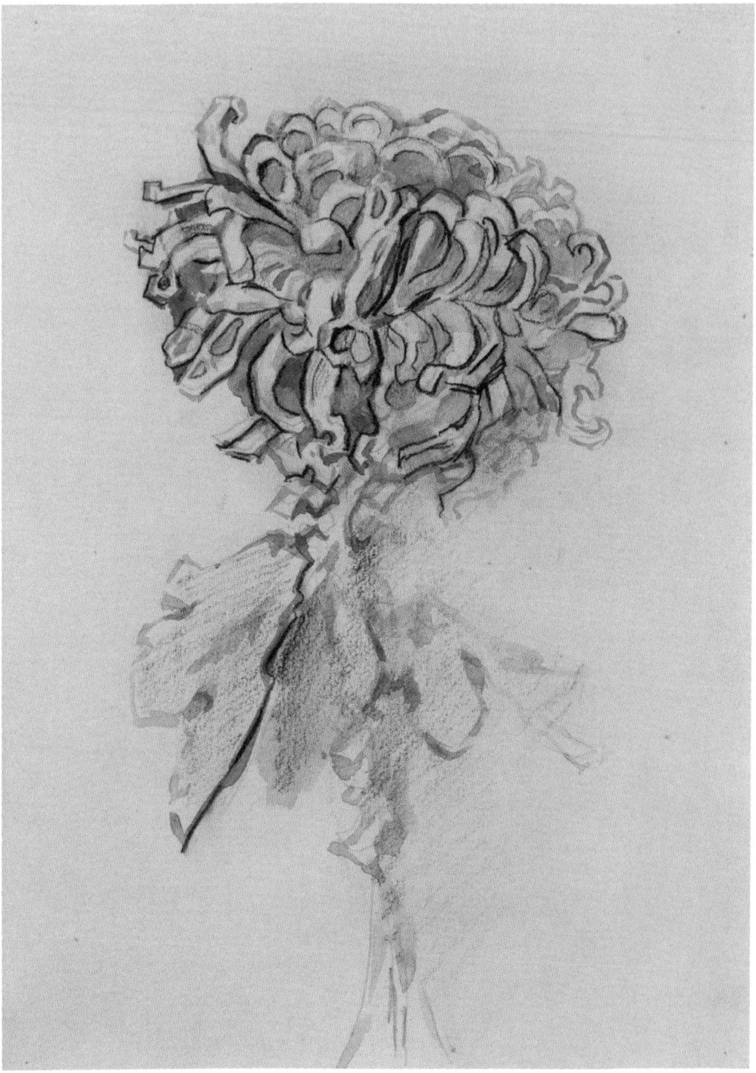

c → Cubism

A brief visit in Paris in May 1911, where he exhibited in the Salon des Indépendants, had reinforced Mondrian's conviction that his project for his art to advance to absolute truth and to abstract from nature more was by no means completed. That was presumably based above all on the impression that the artistic avant-garde in Paris and Cubism in particular made on him. Pablo Picasso and Georges Braque had begun with their Cubism to fragment the visual world and put it back together with multiple perspectives, thus radically calling into question traditional ideas of spatiality and perspective, of lighting, coloration, and brushwork.

Mondrian's first longer stay in Paris began in late 1911 and ended in the summer of 1914; World War I prevented his returning to Paris after a visit in the Netherlands. His patron HP Bremmer had organized an exhibition at the Galerie Walrecht in The Hague with seventeen of the paintings Mondrian had painted in Paris to document his artistic development there: he had become one of the international avant-gardists.

The paintings shown in The Hague make it clear that Mondrian was seeking a path of organic abstraction that can no longer be called "Cubist" in the strict sense. He was now using far fewer radiant colors; shades of ocher and gray now determined the overall impression of his paintings, and the line as such became increasingly important. At first Mondrian was refining the theme of "tree" or "plant" that he had begun in the Netherlands and created paintings in which lines and relatively intricate planes of colors seem to open upward like a funnel. Then he turned to compositions of larger planes. Sketches suggest that in doing so he oriented himself around the traces of rooms that could be seen on the walls of demolished buildings. → see pp. 10/11 His experience with these images enabled him to put representationalism completely behind him. A painting such as *Composition No. IX* of 1913 → p. 19 consists of a structure of nested forms, most of which are determined by the right angle. This results in an impression of space. The viewing eye is kept in constant motion by the contrast of intricate planes and illusionistic space. At the edge of the painting, the configuration seems to get lost in the infinite. He seemed to want to approach the absolute truth as close as possible by means of a painted structure that looks like a manifestation in expansive space.[2]

C *Composition in Brown and Gray / Composition No. IX*
[Gemälde Nr. II / Composition No. IX / Compositie 5] 1913
Oil on canvas 85.7 × 75.6 cm
Museum of Modern Art, New York

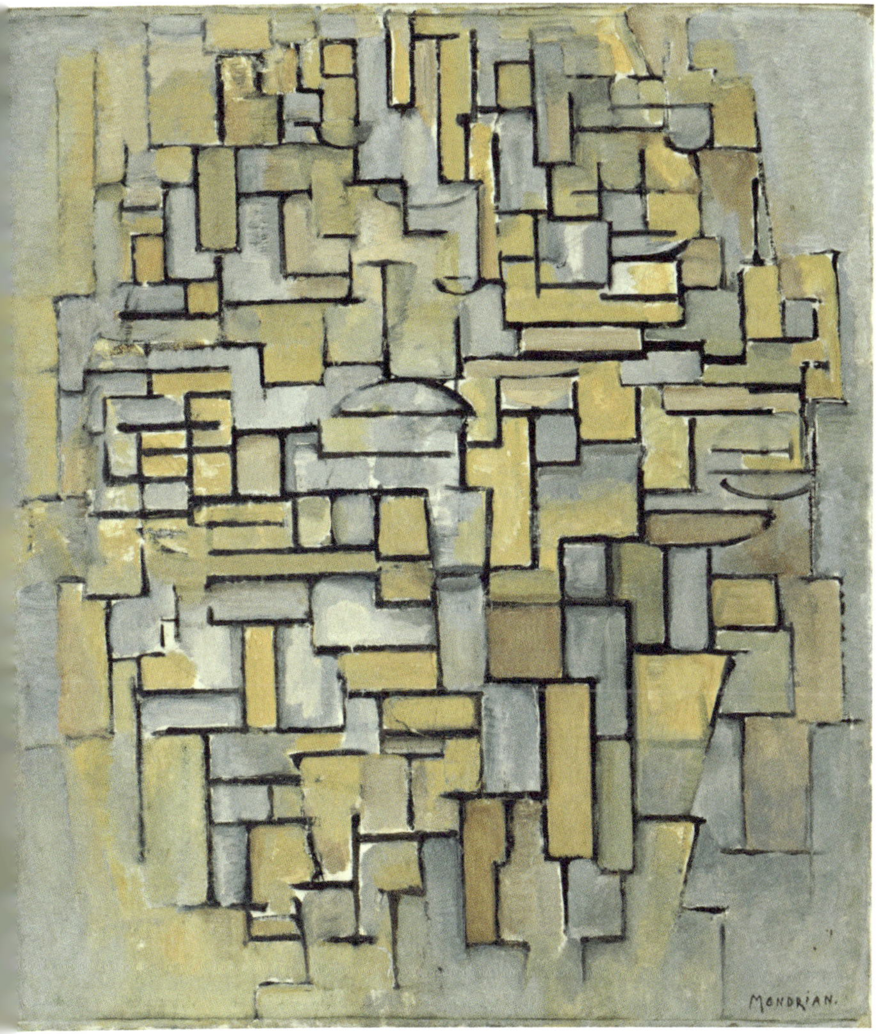

D → Duivendrecht

In early 1905, Mondrian began to paint a series of views of the Weltevrede farm, which was located in a polder landscape from the seventeenth century near Duivendrecht, a town south of Amsterdam that has since grown together with the metropolis. The view through a group of bare trees to the stately house located on the water is a typical Dutch landscape motif.[→Holland] A house for dreaming, beneath a broad sky, atmospheric.

Mondrian later grappled with this motif again, after a first turn to radically nonrepresentational painting.[→Cubism] Between 1914 and 1917, he painted five additional versions of the farm, each time with a different atmosphere of light and color.

Why did Mondrian return to representational painting? First, all of these paintings were probably commissioned works whose sale helped the artist, who was having financial troubles, get by. But that was not all: these works are much too subtly constructed for that. After all, an important element is added to the paintings after 1914 that is often missing in the earlier views: the reflection of the motif in the water. The image is thus repeated within the image, which raises the question: Which is more illusion? The image or the image as mirror image? Especially in the version from around 1916, painted with thin oil paint and now in Chicago, one can see how Mondrian contrasted the planarity of the

D *Farm near Duivendrecht* ca. 1916
Oil on canvas 86.3 × 107.9 cm
The Art Institute of Chicago
Gift of Dolly J. van der Hoop Schoenberg 2001

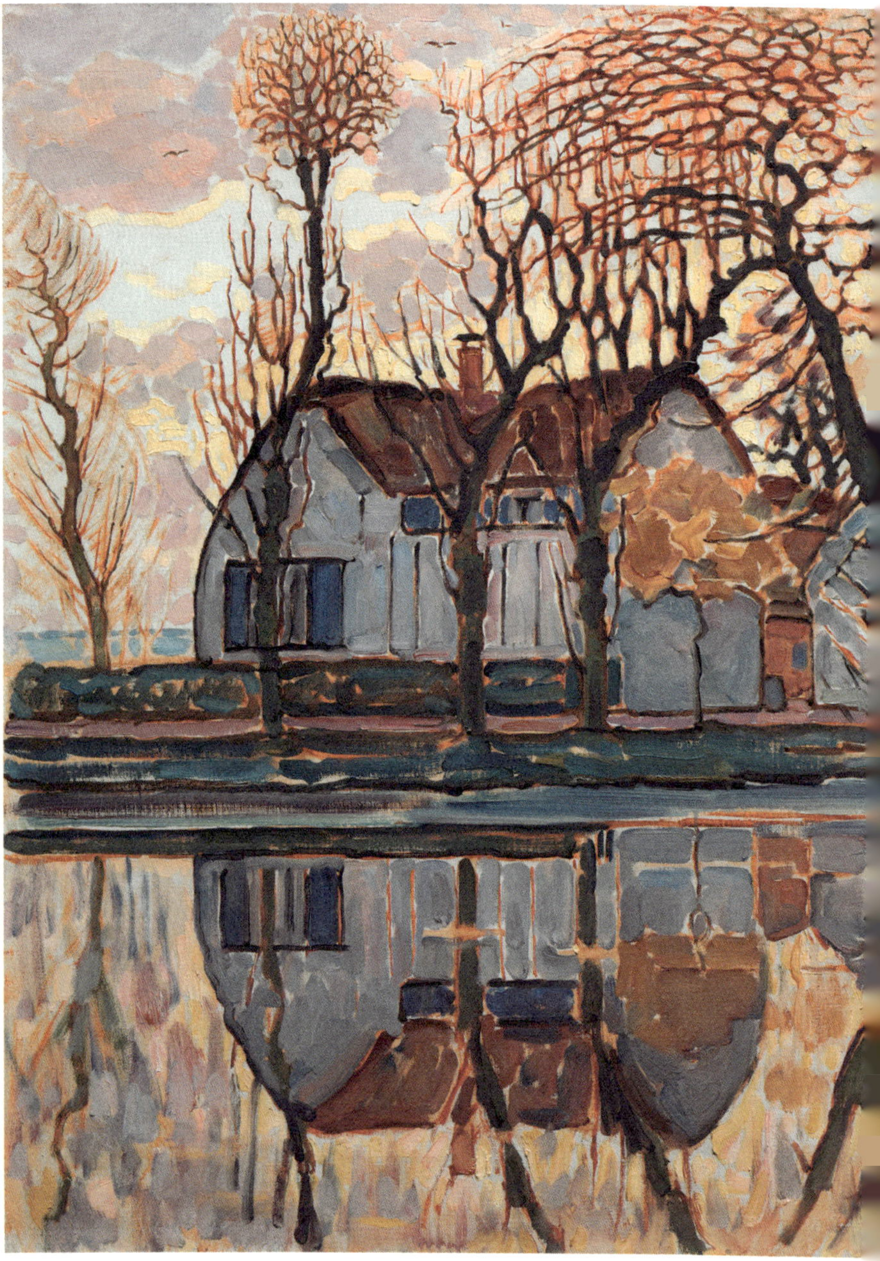

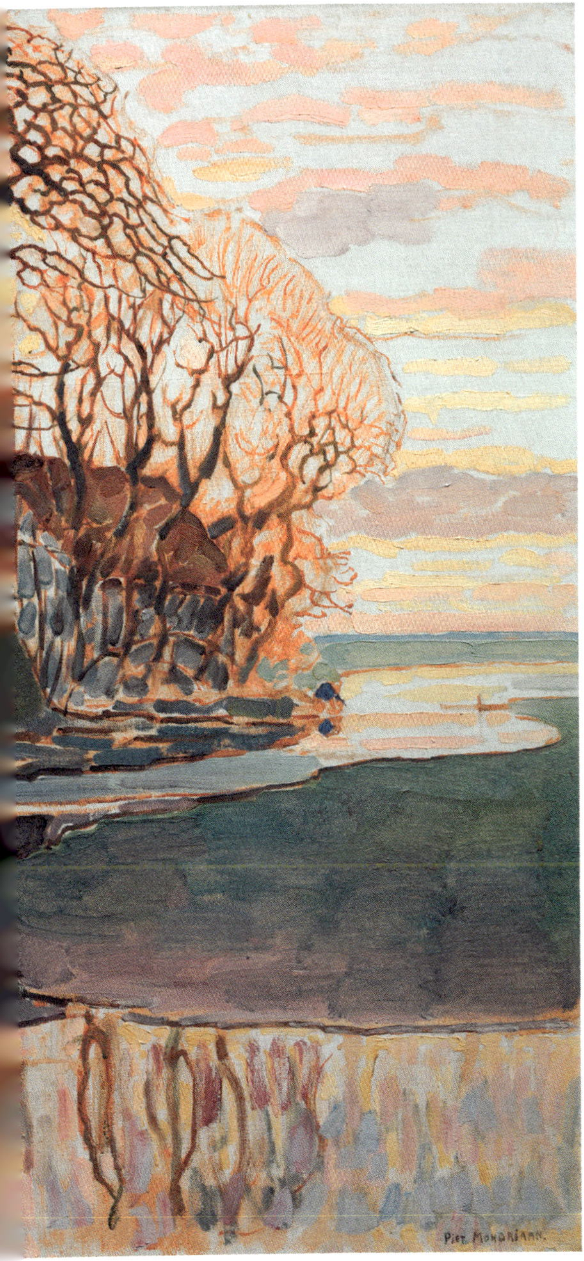
Piet MONDRIAAN.

depiction of the house with the highly stylized structure of the bare tree branches, which looks like a transparent plane. It seems as if Mondrian wanted to try out the possibilities of abstraction →Abstraction in different color atmospheres in order to push ahead to the limits of figuration in the process.

E → Evolution

E *Evolution* 1911
Oil on canvas Triptych: 178 × 85, 183 × 87.5, 178 × 85 cm
Kunstmuseum Den Haag

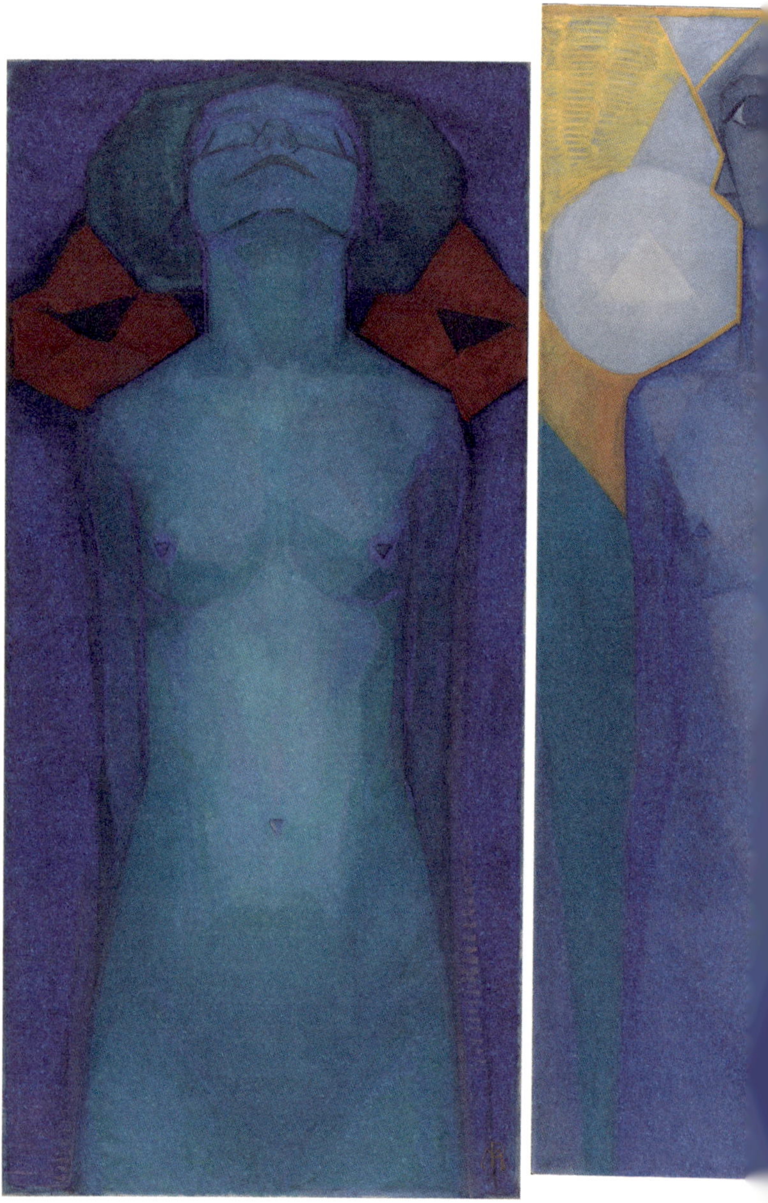

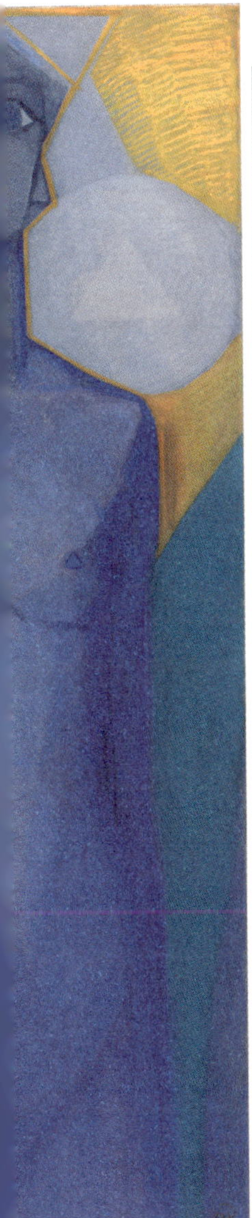

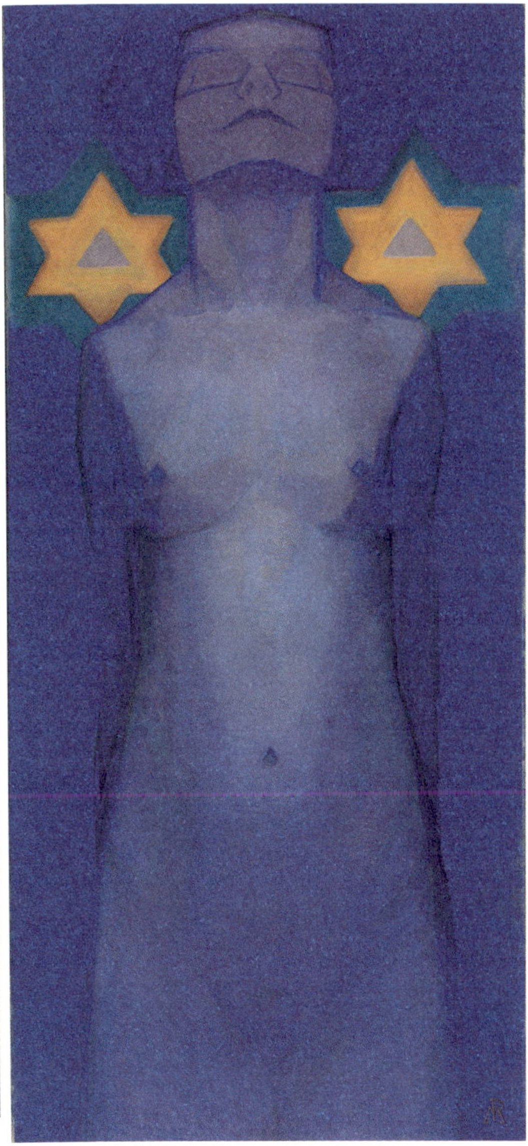

In an exhibition in October 1911 at the Moderne Kunstkring (Modern Art Circle), the art society he had cofounded, Mondrian showed the triptych *Evolution*. This large-format work can be interpreted as a visual realization of central ideas of theosophy, of which Mondrian was an adherent.[→Theosophy] The stylized female nudes on the left and right seem to be still clinging to the earthly. They are sounded by passion flowers and arum. The central figure, with her wide-open eyes, has reached a higher, spiritual sphere; she is surrounded by the light of knowledge and truth. When the triptych is presented, this central painting should be hung higher.

This triptych charged with pathos and meaning is controversial. It is apparently about depicting stages of the evolution of humanity or of the soul:[3] Mondrian himself regarded it rather critically even as he was still completing it, a friend later reported.[4] His wish to depict in a painting the evolution to knowing essential truth presumably did not really work for him here. Reaching a higher-level "truth" by means of ever more radical abstraction of nature nevertheless remained a central maxim of Mondrian's artistic activity.[→Abstraction] He liked to use the term "evolution"—though not in Charles Darwin's sense. For Mondrian, "evolution" meant acquiring experiences on which one could build a new level of artistic experience in order to obtain expanded knowledge.

F → Foxtrot

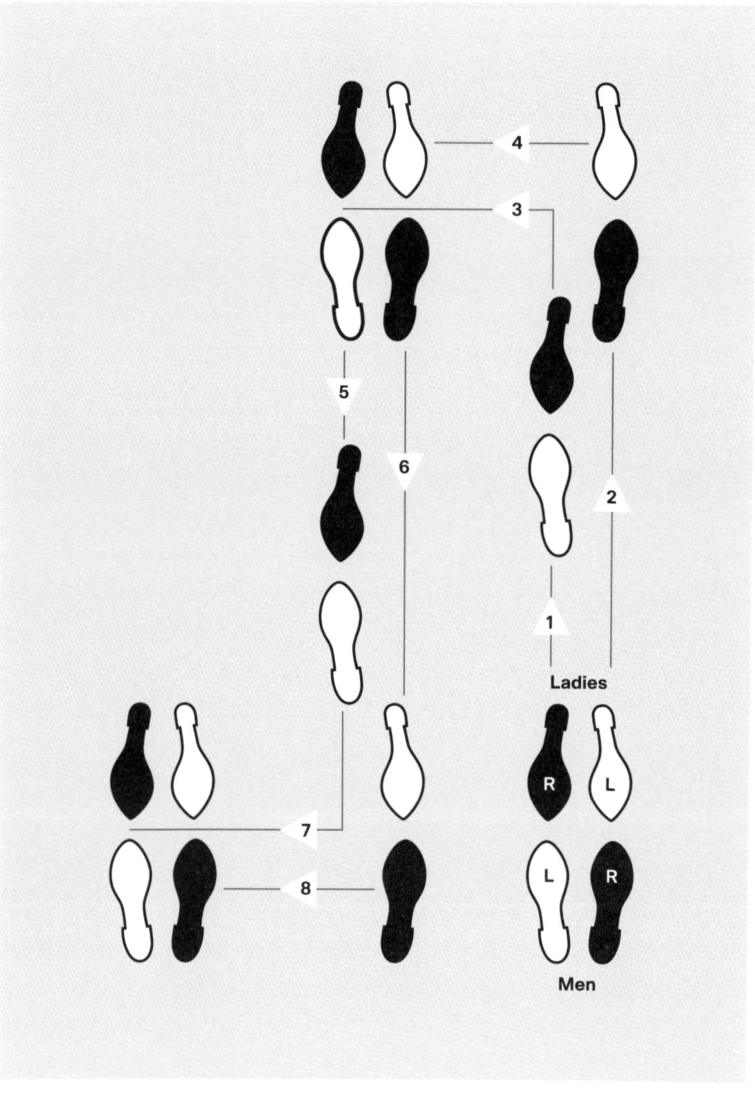

4
3
5
6
2
1
Ladies
R
L
L
R
7
8
Men

Piet Mondrian liked to spend his evenings and nights in dance clubs. That does not fit with the image many have of him, believing that a painter of such seemingly "strict" paintings must have been an ascetic who lived like a monk. Mondrian was an enthusiastic dancer, and he must have been just as innovative when inventing dance moves as he was in his art. That is what has been said by the painter Lee Krasner, who had met Mondrian in New York in the early 1940s and liked to go dancing with him.→Krasner

Mondrian saw a direct connection between dance and painting. The critic Augustine de Meester-Obreen wrote in 1919 that she had once asked Mondrian in a room full of dancing people how he would paint such a party, to which he replied that he would abstract this impression and depict it as vertical and horizontal lines.[5]

One of the dances that Mondrian especially liked was the foxtrot, which he encountered in Paris after 1919. Looking at the sequence of basic steps makes it clear why: the foxtrot is a dance of vertical and horizontal movements across the floor. There are no diagonals like those in the Viennese waltz. If one views Mondrian's paintings intensely, especially those from around or just after 1920, for example, *Tableau No. I*,→p. 46 one gets a sense of where the correspondence between dance and painting might lie. Like dance, paintings have a basic form that is never precisely repeated but is similar. The freedom of the dancers to vary the basic steps corresponds to different weighting of colors and the size of color fields in paintings. There is often a regular element and an irregular one in the structure of Mondrian's paintings. The regular contrasts with the irregular, which would not exist without the regular. This conveys a rhythm →Rhythm on which all of Mondrian's nonrepresentational paintings are based.

G → Gein

G *Trees on the Gein: Moonrise*
[Five Tree Silhouettes along the Gein with Moon] 1907–08
Oil on canvas 79 × 92.5 cm
Kunstmuseum Den Haag

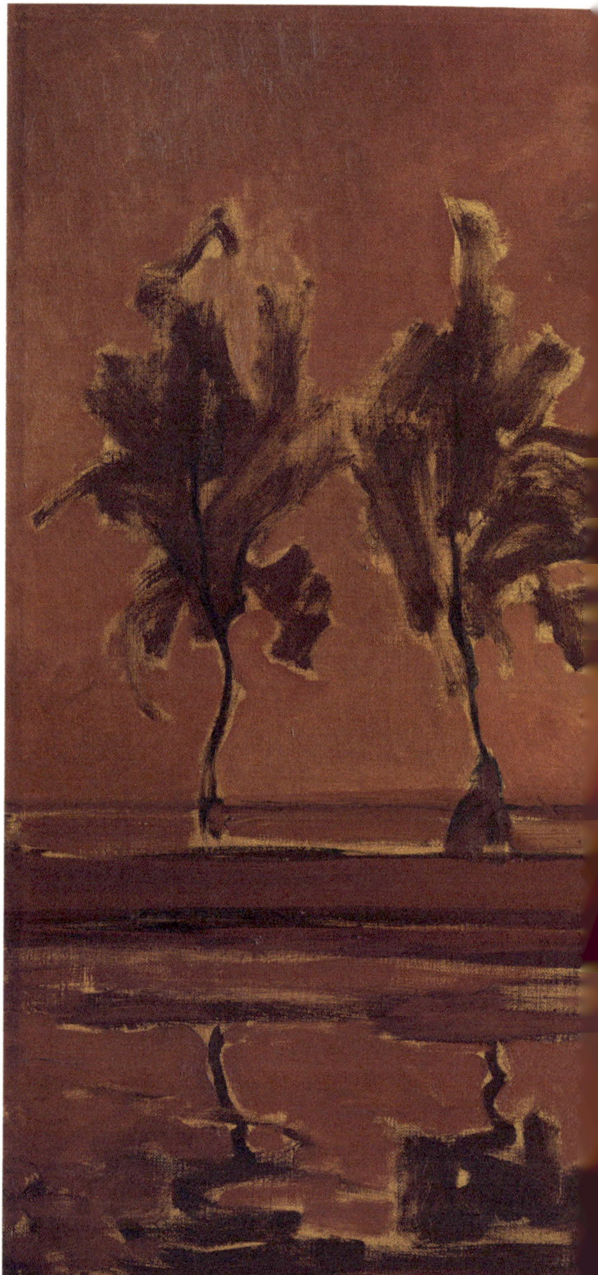

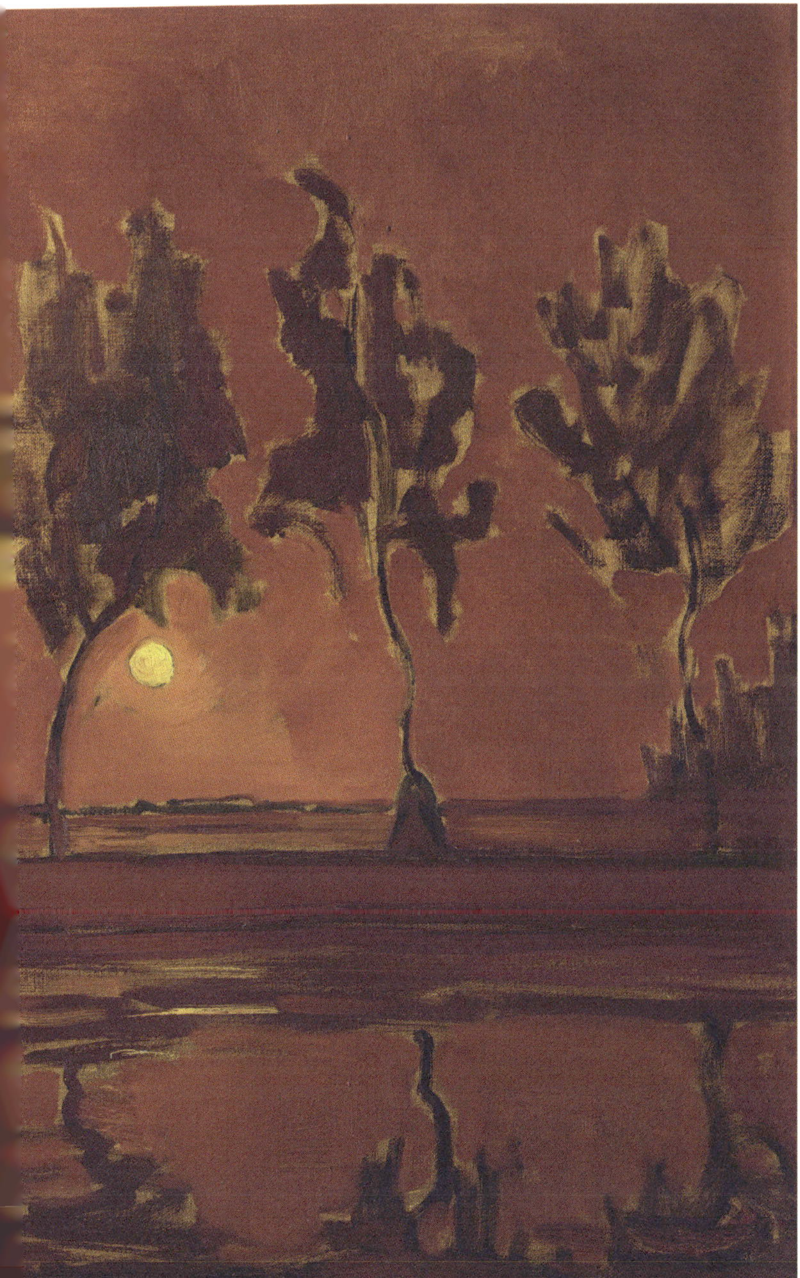

The Gein is a waterway in southeast Amsterdam that is part of the complex and very old canal system that characterizes Amsterdam itself but also its environs.

Mondrian frequently visited and often painted this landscape; especially impressive are his paintings from around 1907, a year in which the artist experimented a great deal with the elements of painting: the use of color, the relationship of line and form, and so on. Many of the experiences he gained and then employed can also be recognized in the later nonrepresentational paintings.

Consider, for example, a sketch-like painting entirely in shades of reddish-brown: *Trees on the Gein: Moonrise* of 1907, where five trees are standing on a dike backlit by the full moon. The plane extends to the horizon; water is depicted in the foreground, and the trees are reflected in it. Rows of trees by the water can be seen everywhere in Holland;→Holland they are a popular motif of Impressionist landscape painting. One need only think of Claude Monet's paintings of rows of poplars.

Mondrian's composition is based on a simple idea that he employed almost exclusively from about 1919–20 at the latest, apart from the realistic flower paintings he painted now and again thereafter: Vertical lines, in this case trees, meet a horizontal one, here the dike. The picture is determined by the right angle and by the repetition of trees, which could be continued into infinity. As regular as it looks as a whole, there are deviations: the form of the trees varies, which results in a kind of rhythm →Rhythm so in the painting, as if the trees were dancing. The moon in particular brings an element of irregularity into place: it is the Romantic moon of nineteenth-century art. On the one hand, Mondrian is putting himself in the tradition of Dutch landscape painting; on the other, the structure of his painting points far into the future of his art.

H → Holland

Holland, which is composed of the provinces of Noord- and Zuid-Holland and includes the cities Amsterdam, The Hague, and Rotterdam, is located in the west of the Netherlands on the North Sea. Large parts of Holland are located below sea level and result from centuries of land reclamation by means of dikes. The resulting tracts of land are called polders; they have to be drained constantly via canals. The water is led via channels to slightly higher canals and riverways by which it flows away. For a long time, this was achieved by means of Archimedean screws driven by windmills. If one looks at the polder landscape from above, for example, when flying to Amsterdam, the polders recall Mondrian's abstract paintings, which appear to be composed just as "strictly" and regularly.

Piet Mondrian, who was from the Dutch province of Utrecht, where he was born in Amersfoort on March 7, 1872, was not from Holland, but in his early period he was an important painter of the characteristic landscape of Holland. Landscape is the opposite of nature: whereas nature is subject to the principle of constant change, landscape is nature designed by human beings and is supposed to change only slowly, if at all. Piet Mondrian often painted this elaborately designed landscape with its channels, canals, and mills. A good example of that is the painting *The Oostzijdse Mill along the River Gein by Moonlight.* →Gein One sees here the land to the left of Gein, which is somewhat lower and is being

H *Oostzijdse Mill along the River Gein by Moonlight* ca. 1903
Oil on canvas 63 × 75.4 cm
Rijksmuseum, Amsterdam

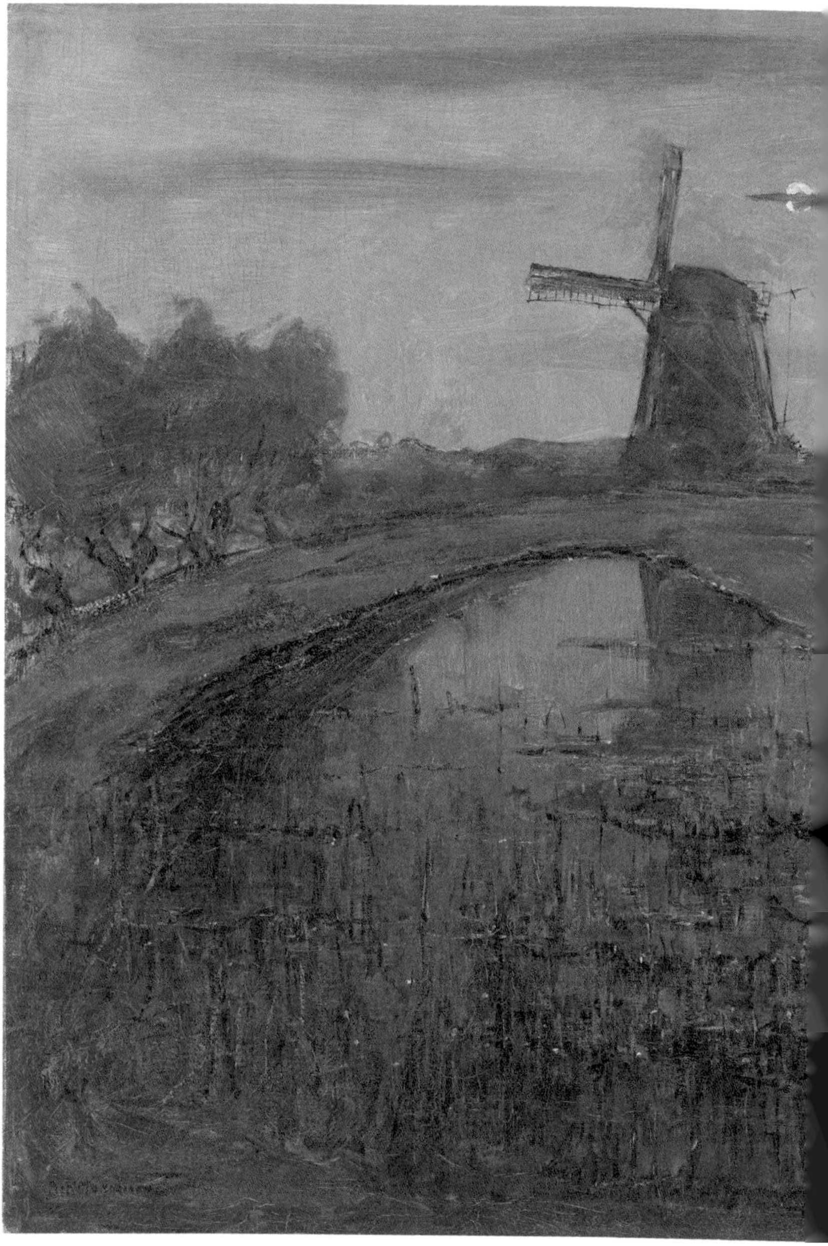

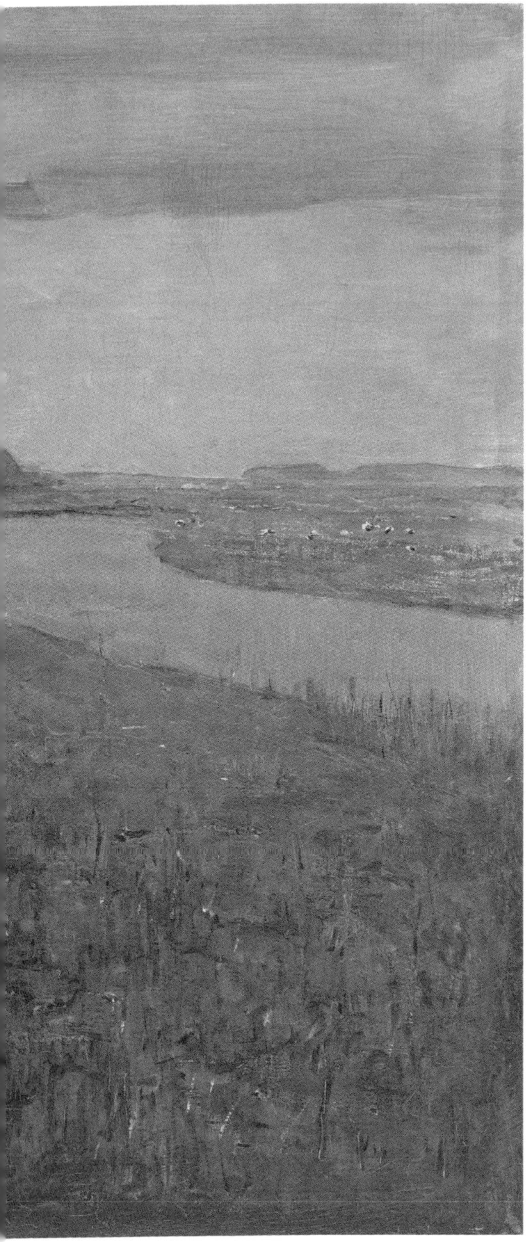

H Still there today: the Oostzijdse Mill at the River Gein near Abcoude. Photograph by Ulf Küster, November 2021

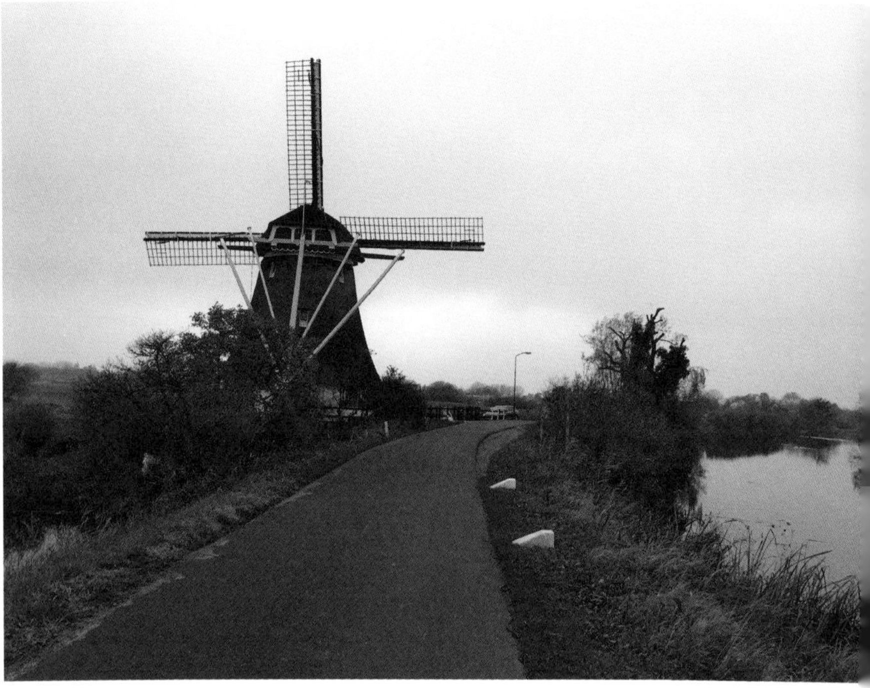

drained with the aid of the windmill. Was Mondrian aware that he was depicting something very artificial in his art? The view that Mondrian painted still exists today.

I → Intuition and Precision

At first glance Piet Mondrian's abstract paintings look as if they had been designed at the drawing board; that is how precise and exact they seem. When one studies them more closely, it turns out that no painting is like any other. This is most evident if one looks at the painter's repetitions of his own compositions: these paintings resemble one another, but they are not copies. No exactly geometrically measurable relationships can be shown between the individual color fields in his paintings. Mondrian clearly always relied on his artistic intuition when designing his compositions. And, especially astonishingly, he seems to have used a ruler or straightedge only very rarely if at all to draw his black lines—or at least that has not been proven yet.

This is the information and the results of the research of the conservators of the Fondation Beyeler, who have examined all seven of Mondrian's works in the Beyeler Collection.[6] Under the microscope, the black lines do not look so exact at all. Nevertheless, he must have had an extraordinarily steady hand when painting. It is notable in this context that not only the planes of color but also the black lines are composed of several superimposed layers, probably in order to produce as deep a black as possible. How did he manage to create the impression of precision despite having freely "composed" the paintings?

The Fondation Beyeler has the work *Tableau No. I*, which Mondrian began in 1921, or perhaps already

I *Tableau No. I*
[Composition/Tableau No. I, with Red, Blue, Yellow, Black, and Gray]
ca. 1920–25
Oil on canvas 75.5 × 65.5 cm
Fondation Beyeler, Beyeler Collection, Riehen/Basel

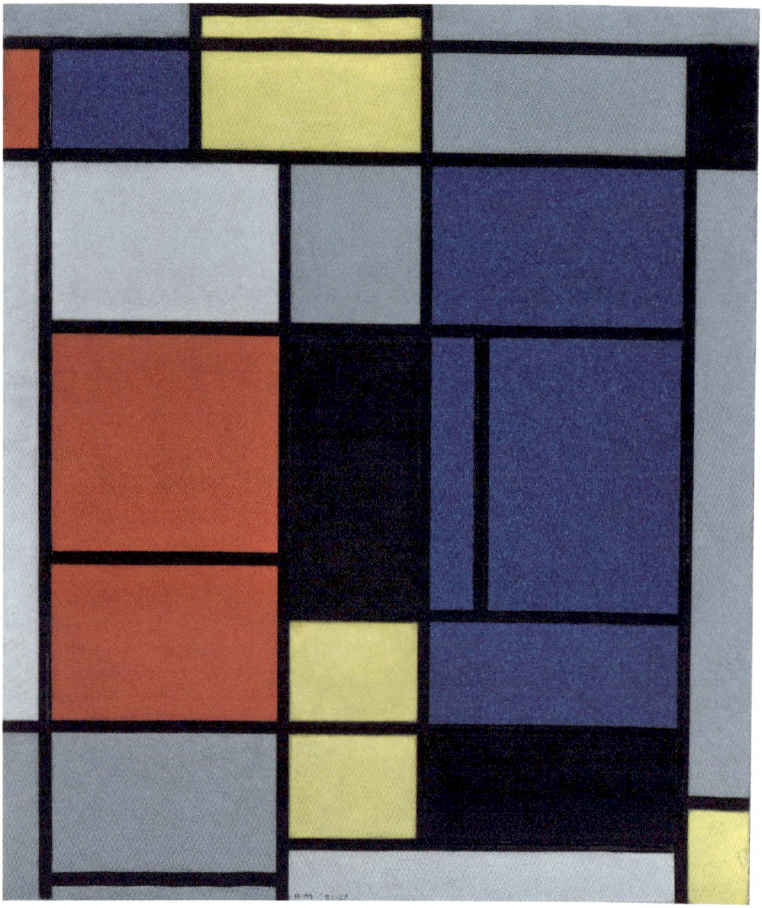

I Infrared image of *Tableau No. I*
It reveals the grid on which the composition of the painting is based

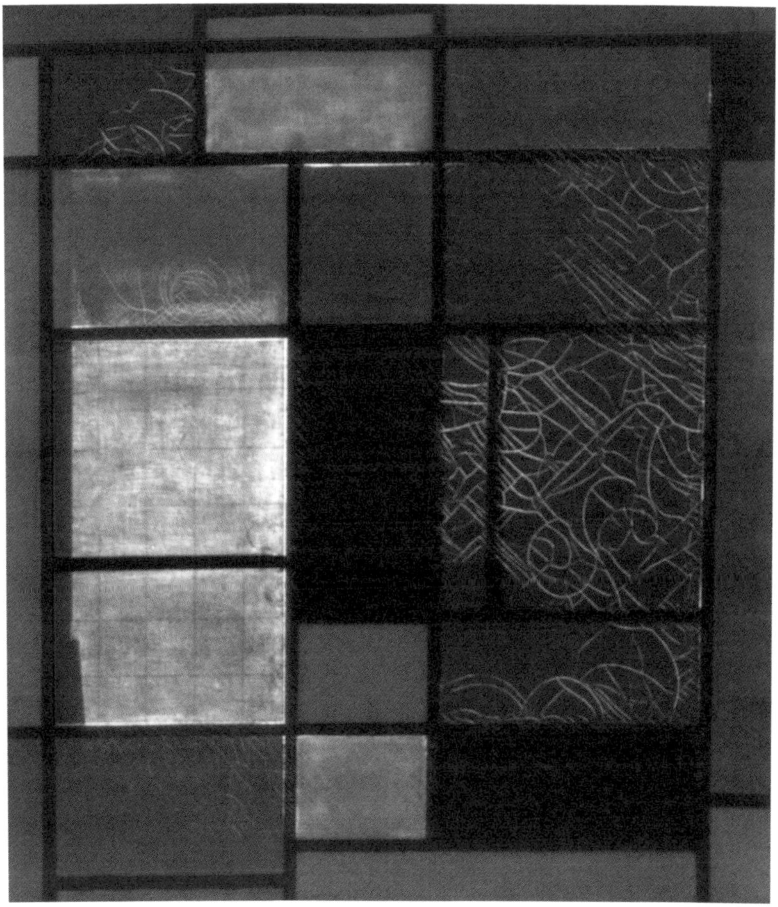

in 1920, but did not complete until 1925.→p. 46 Infrared and X-ray analyses have shown that he used charcoal to underdraw a kind of grid on the ground.→p. 47 When filling in with black oil paint the lines that delimit the planes of color, he largely followed this grid, which probably had been drawn with a ruler.

Mondrian had experience with grid pictures in earlier years. Under the paint layer of his late abstract paintings, there are only summary preparatory drawings in charcoal with which the position of the black lines was established vertically or horizontally. That presumably means that with practice Mondrian became increasingly confident and freer in the composition of his paintings. And with that his painting technique grew ever more precise (and probably also slower). Intuition and precision are closely connected in Mondrian's work.

J → Jazz

Mondrian's interest in music seems to have developed in parallel with the "evolution" →Evolution of his art from figuration to abstraction. In his Amsterdam studio, where he worked from 1908 to 1911, a laurel-wreathed death mask of Beethoven was hanging, and he is said to have listened to Richard Wagner as well. His friendship with the composer Jakob van Domselaer, who was influenced by Arnold Schoenberg and whom he met in 1912, opened up the world of the musical avant-garde for him. At the same time the dancing fan Mondrian →Foxtrot was interested in early forms of jazz, above all ragtime. His encounter with jazz, which American soldiers brought to Paris after World War I, reinforced him in his view that the music of Neoplasticism, the radical new art movement he was propagating, →Nieuwe Beelding would emerge from avant-garde music and jazz. What fascinated him about jazz was its break from traditional conventions, its regular basic form, and the opportunities to move away from it by means of syncopated rhythms and improvisation; he saw parallels to his own work.[7]

In New York, to which he emigrated in 1940, Mondrian experienced jazz again in an entirely new way: he was particularly enthusiastic about boogie-woogie. When he had guests—and perhaps at other times as well—he liked to play boogie-woogie records on his gramophone. He was inspired by this music to make his final group of works, an evolution →Evolution

J For the painter Gwen Lux, Mondrian plays the latest records on his gramophone in his studio, 1934

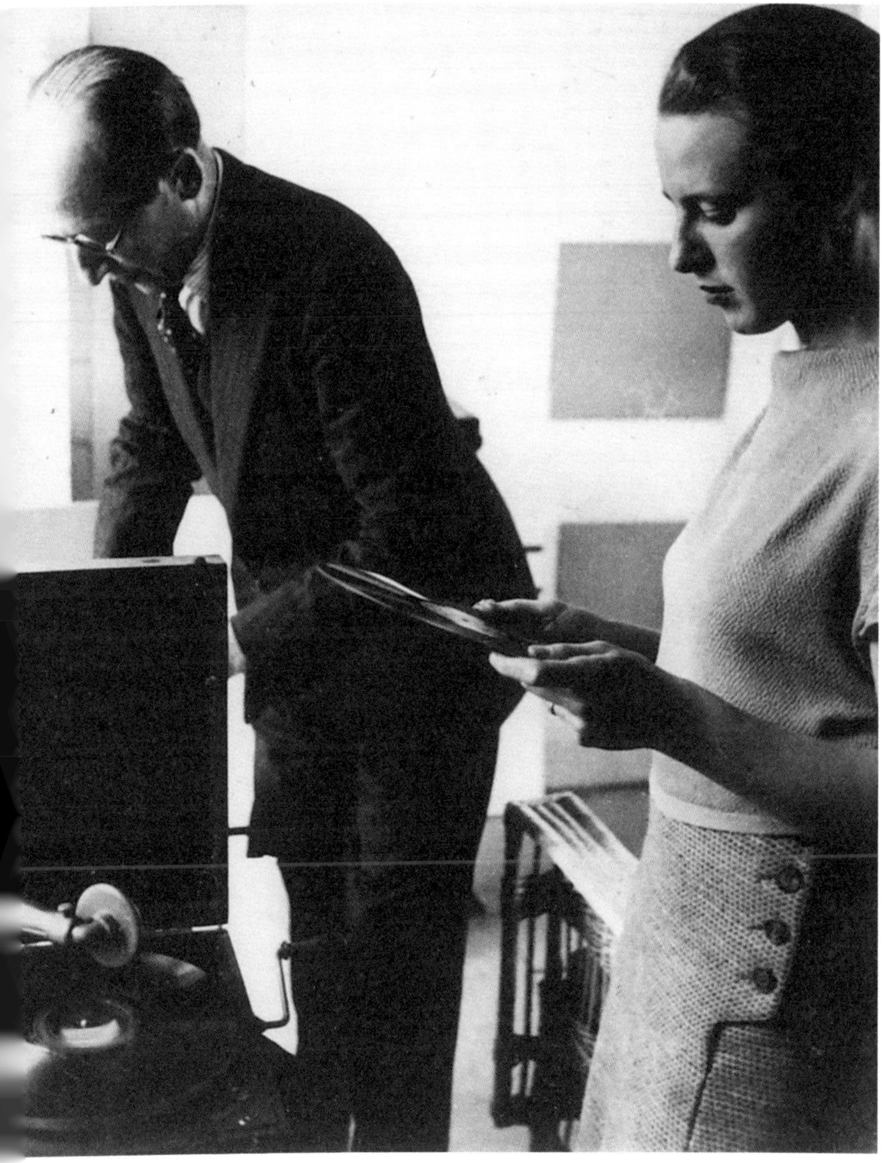

J *Victory Boogie Woogie* 1942–44
Oil, tape, paper, charcoal, and pencil on canvas
178.4 × 178.4 cm (measured diagonally)
Kunstmuseum Den Haag

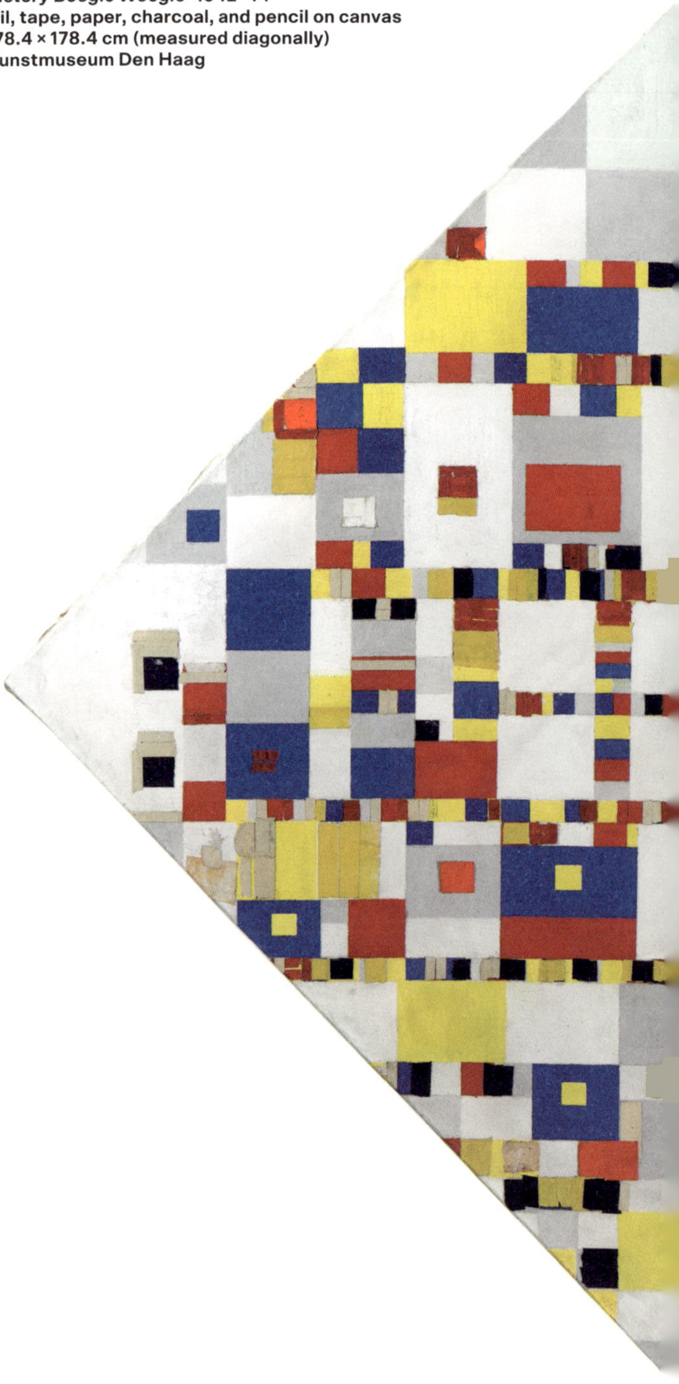

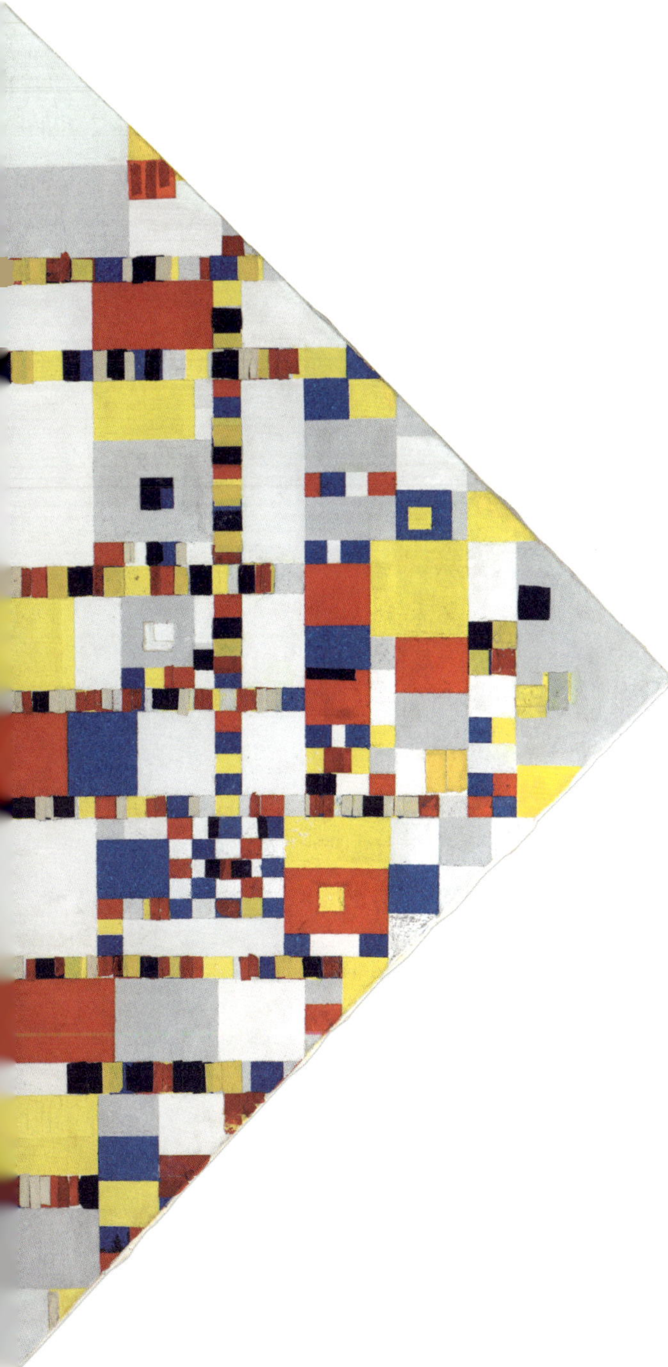

of his Neoplastic style. In these paintings the black disappears under dividing lines that are now made of colorful rectangles and in part collaged. The areas of color between them are much smaller and composed of several superimposed areas. When looking at these paintings—for example, *Victory Boogie Woogie*, the making of which was interrupted by his death—in a concentrated way and following the interlocking lines in the painting, a kind of visual staccato results, a rhythm that can be associated with the rhythm of boogie-woogie.

K→ Lee Krasner

When Piet Mondrian arrived in New York on October 3, 1940, he seemingly had no difficulty at all gaining a foothold in the art world. As an avant-gardist he was already almost a legend, and despite his advanced age—he was approaching seventy—he was admired as a role model by younger artists in particular. One of these was the painter Lee Krasner (1908–1984), who was long overshadowed by her future husband, Jackson Pollock. Mondrian also appreciated Krasner. It has been suggested that Mondrian may have been inspired by Krasner's collages for his late experiments with tape and collage.[8] The two also went dancing together; according to Krasner, who considered herself a fairly good dancer, it was not always easy to follow Mondrian's improvised steps.[9]

Krasner herself experienced and never forgot that Mondrian was able to encourage younger artists. Both attended the exhibition *American Abstract Artists* in 1941, which showed works by him as well as by her. When Mondrian saw Krasner's paintings, he said to her: "You have a very strong inner rhythm. You must always hold that."[10] His remark was simply "beautiful," Krasner said; despite her paintings had curved forms, she said, so that they were entirely different from the paintings of her colleague.

K Lee Krasner in her studio ca. 1945

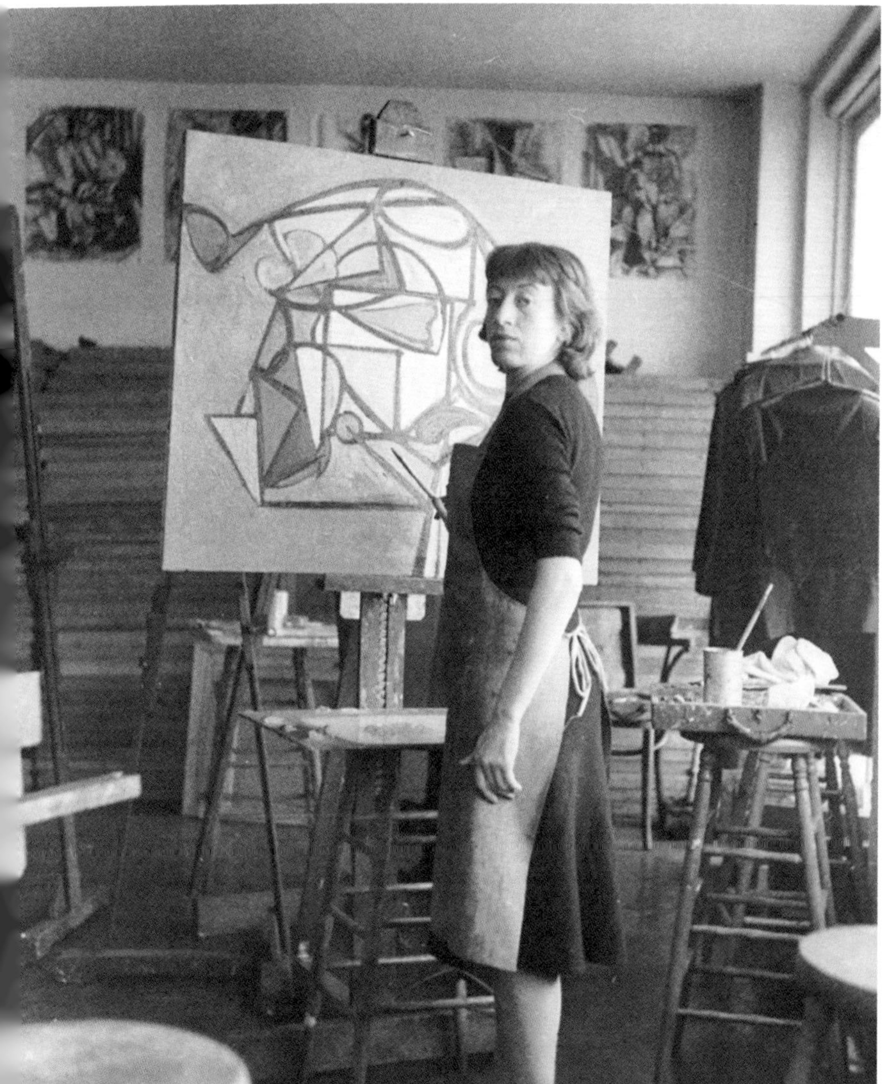

L → Love

Mondrian loved many women, and many women loved Mondrian. That is still surprising to those who believe that an artist who made such abstract art could only dedicate himself exclusively to art—although they are thinking only of the later, nonrepresentational paintings with right angles. The apparent discrepancy between the effect of his art and his nature was not easy for his contemporaries to understand either. An unnamed Russian poet who was talking about abstract art with Mondrian and went dancing with him is said to have cried out when faced with the sparseness of his studio: "Mais . . . on ne peut pas faire l'amour ici" (But . . . we can't make love here). For Mondrian, of course, his paintings were not "strict"; they were approaching the essential, the absolute. And for him that had a great deal to do with passion and emotion. Basically, however, his love of art was greater than his love of women. He is said to have been very charming, enjoyed flirting, and was as experimental in his love life and relationships as he was in his art.

To bring a little order into the overwhelming network of Mondrian's many friendships and affairs, the Kunstmuseum Den Haag published a quartet of card games titled *Love Inspiration: The Women of Piet Mondrian*.

Thirteen groups of four characterize the types of relationships between Mondrian and the women, distinguishing between "Family," "Lovers,"

L The charming Piet Mondrian with the painter Gwen Lux
1934

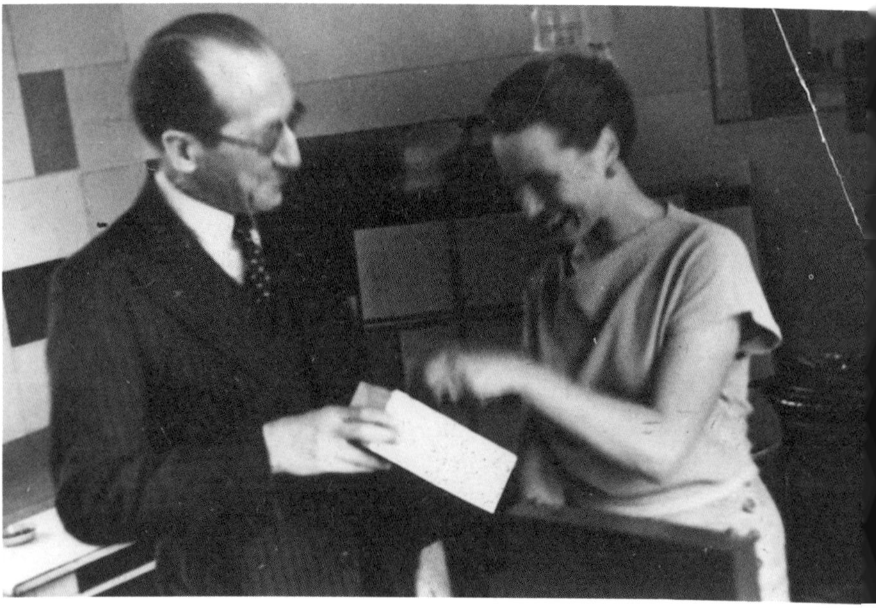

“Admirers,” “Supporters and Advisors,” “Night Strollers,” “Colleagues,” “Girls” (his term for his female drawing students), “Friends of Music,” “Collectors,” “Women with whom he stayed,” “PR women who promoted him,” “Women of the beau monde,” and “Dance Partners.” Belonging to one category did not rule out belonging to another as well.

Mondrian was engaged twice: first to Greta Heijbroek, with whom he broke up when he moved to Paris at the end of 1911. And at the age of fifty-six, when he fell in love with Lily Bles, the eighteen-year-old daughter of the poet Dop Bles. The relationship lasted two years; they wanted to marry. Mondrian even purchased a large bed and built a cradle, but Lily’s parents vetoed it.

M → Frits Mondriaan, Piet Mondriaan Sr., and the Maris Family of Painters

In New York in 1941, in his booklet *Toward the True Vision of Reality* about his first art teachers, Mondrian wrote: "I began to paint at an early age. My first teachers were my father, an amateur, and my uncle, a professional painter."[11]

Mondrian did not by any means grow up in a milieu unfamiliar with art. But his memory is not quite correct: uncle Frits, too, was an amateur, because he had taken over the family's perfume and wig company in The Hague. He was, however, quite successful as a painter and is associated with the Hague school of painters: Dutch landscape painting influenced by Impressionism. Pieter Cornelis Mondriaan Sr.—Frits's brother and Mondrian's father—was a teacher and talented at drawing. His son also became a teacher, specifically a teacher of drawing. It was presumably a problem for the father that this profession did not satisfy Piet junior and he wanted to study art at the academy, which would have posed a financial problem, as his father probably feared.[12]

One of the leading painters of the Hague school, and probably the most innovative one, because of his light-flooded paintings, was Willem Maris (1844–1910). He was presumably an important role model for a long time. It was difficult for Mondrian to get free of him. Maris's son Simon, who was also a painter, was a friend of Mondrian, and the two of them traveled together to Spain in 1903.

M Willem Maris (left), drawing. Mondrian is sitting in the center of this photograph, taken ca. 1900–02 (photographer unknown) . Is Maris drawing Mondrian's portrait?

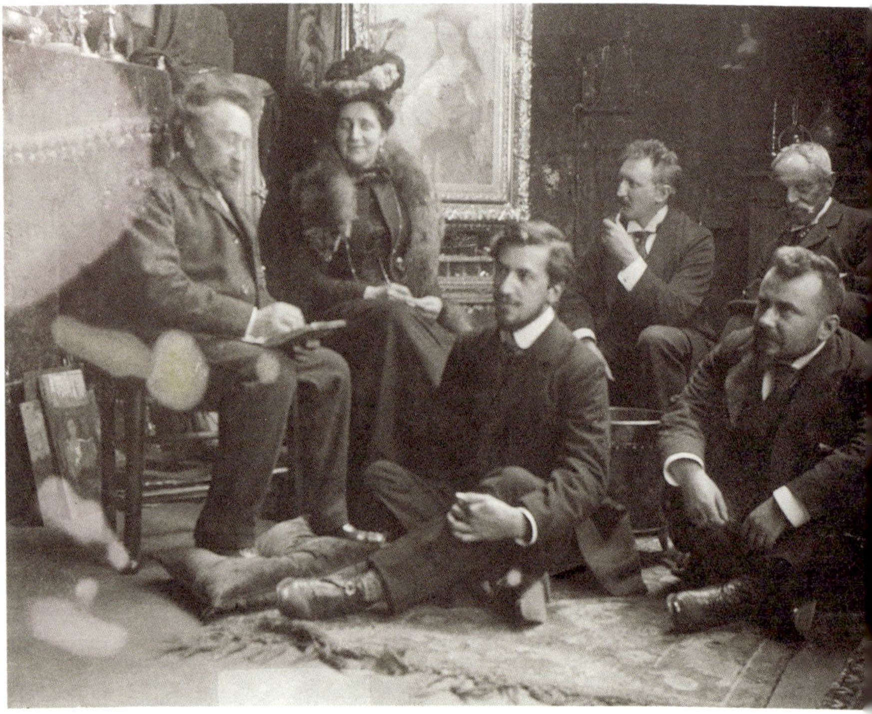

M Simon Maris *Mondrian Painting on a Stationary Bicycle* ca. 1906

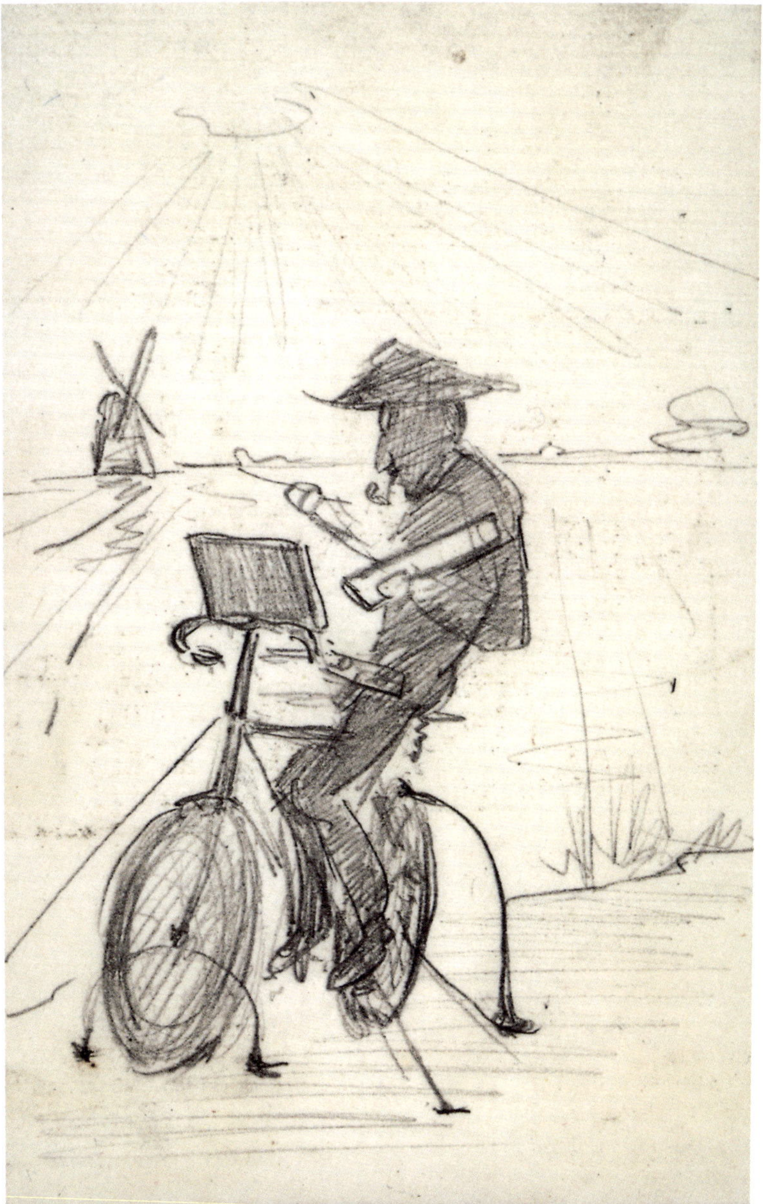

N →

Nieuwe Beelding
Neoplasticism

Mondrian is still associated above all with the abstract works that he painted from around 1920 onward. In his theoretical writings, which first appeared in the journal *De Stijl*,→De Stijl he tried to justify his views. Inspired by his encounter with the philosophy and theosophist Mathieu Hubertus Josephus Schoenmaekers (1875–1944), he had originally called his new means of artistic expression "Nieuwe Beelding," or the new plastic art. In his essays written in French and English, he coined the terms "Néoplasticisme" and "Neoplasticism." It remains difficult to explain what exactly he meant by that.[13] In any case, Neoplasticism was to penetrate all areas of life. For Mondrian, it expressed another step toward abstraction,→Abstraction in order to advance to the absolute, whatever that meant to him.

In practical terms, Neoplasticism meant concentrating on the essential means of painting: on the one hand, the "noncolors," black and white, on opposite ends of the color scale. On the other hand, the primary colors yellow, red, and blue, which did not necessarily have to appear together in the painting. As a rule, the lines are black and run vertically and horizontally and form right angles where they meet, just as human beings and plants (vertical) stand on the earth (horizontal). The right angle defines and delimits planes, which are either white or formed by the primary colors. No painting is symmetrical. They are designed as planes, even if the combinations of colors can evoke the impression

N *Composition with Yellow and Blue* 1932
Oil on canvas 55.5 × 55.5 cm
Fondation Beyeler, Beyeler Collection, Riehen/Basel

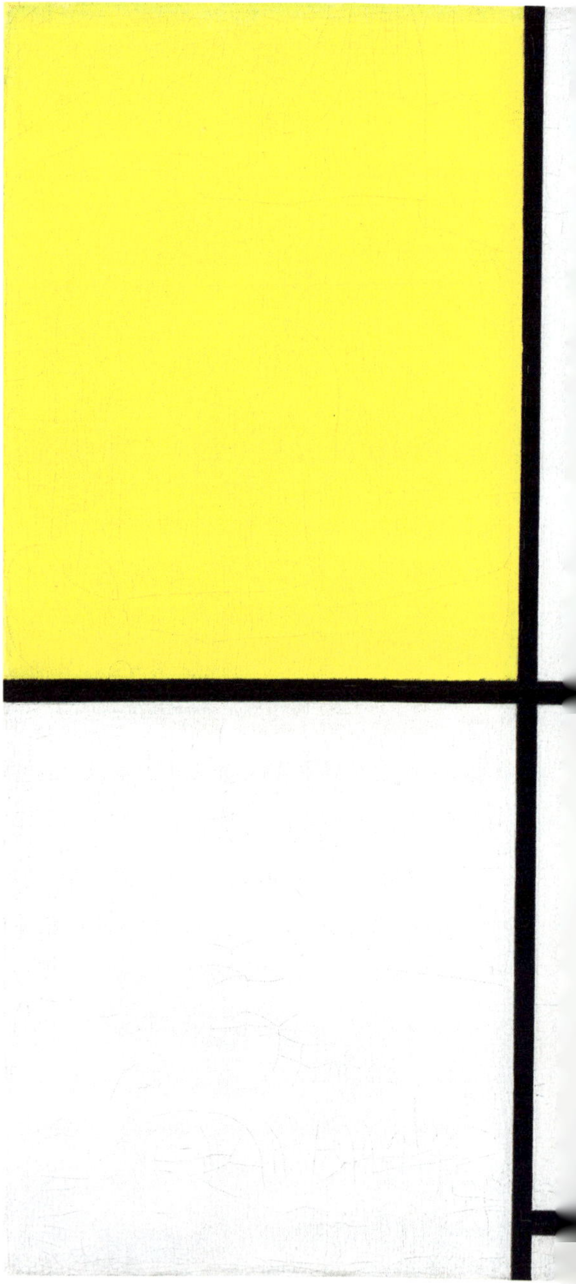

P M 32

of spatiality. Ideally, a spiritual space should emerge between the paintings of Neoplasticism and the viewers.

The possibilities of compositions based on the interplay of all these factors are infinite. Mondrian was concerned with creating a perfect equilibrium that nevertheless has tension and in which all of the elements appear to be in their proper place. That is why it is easy to recognize, once one has studied intensely, when one of his paintings is upside down; it simply doesn't look "right."

0 → Ocean and Pier

On July 25, 1914, Piet Mondrian traveled from Paris to the Netherlands in order to take a brief vacation and visit his father, who had turned sixty-five in June. He also wanted to see his exhibition at the Galerie Walrecht in The Hague once again.→Cubism

On July 28, 1914, World War I began. The Dutch remained neutral, but Germany's occupation of Belgium made it impossible for Mondrian to return to Paris. He was not able to return to his studio in Paris until 1919. Many of the paintings he had begun remained there, as did his paints.

Was it because he was seeking a contrast to urban life and wanted to grapple with the climate of the sea? In any case, he began depicting the sea—for the first time probably in Scheveningen,[14] then in Domburg on the Walcheren Peninsula. In the latter, he had previously painted the expanse of the sea in the years prior to 1911, contrasting it with the breakwaters and piers, which are more or less visible depending on the tide. The constantly changing landscape of dunes in the sometimes large-format paintings and the lighthouses and the church of Domburg were common motifs in brilliant colors at that time.

Now he left the color out and, setting out from his experiences in Paris,→Cubism concentrated on charcoal. He was trying to capture the structure of what he saw, and so he drew the

O *Ocean 4* 1914
Charcoal on paper 50.4 × 62.6 cm
Sammlung E. W. K., Bern

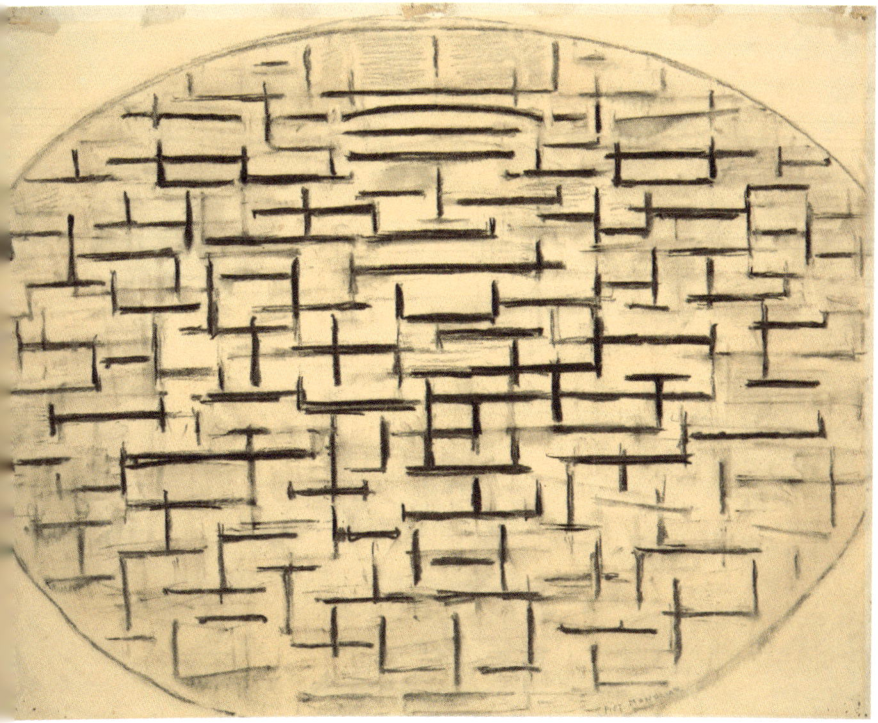

constantly moving sea and the broad sky above it, and the starry firmament at night with the piers and breakwaters looming into the ocean as an (often symmetrical) system of horizontal and vertical lines, most of which meet at right angles. The recumbent oval of his drawings conveys the ocean's enormous size.

P → Paris, London, New York: Three Studios

P Charles Karsten, Piet Mondrian in his studio
Paris, October 1933

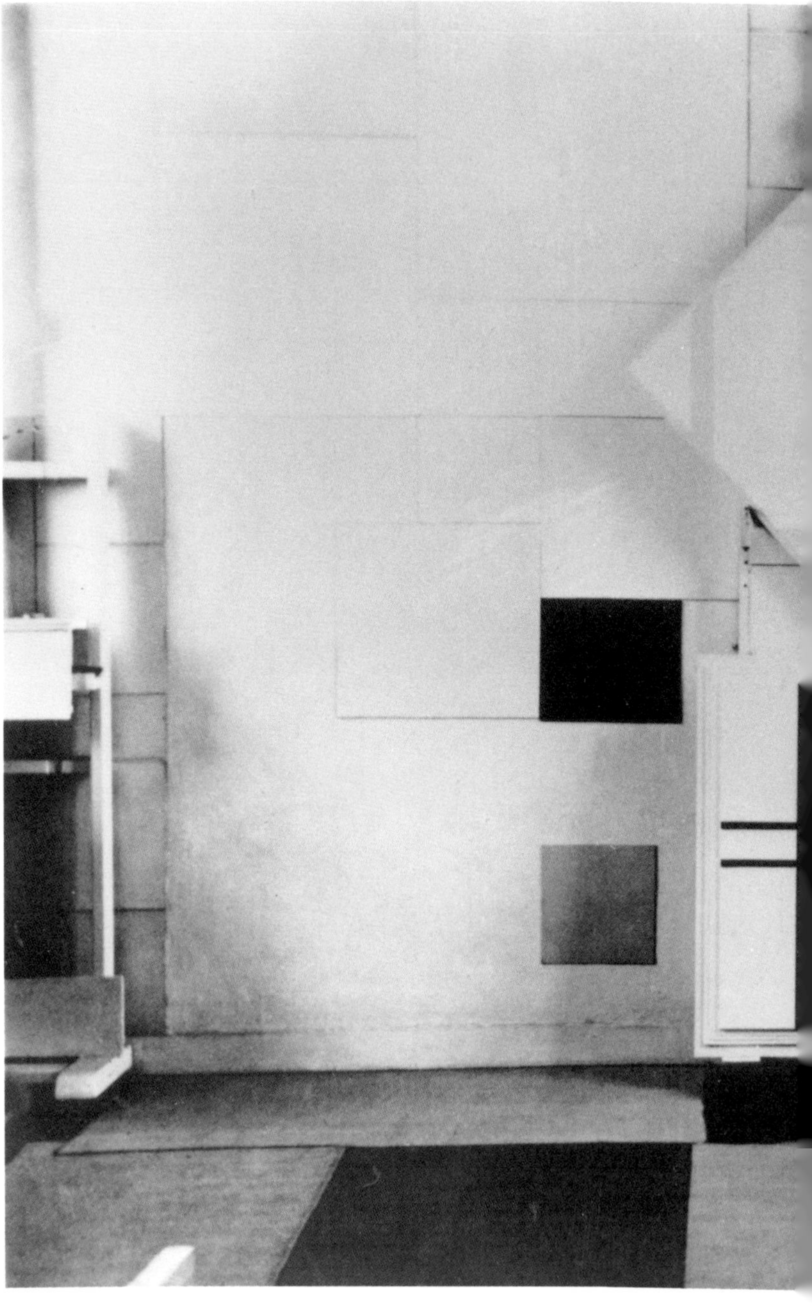

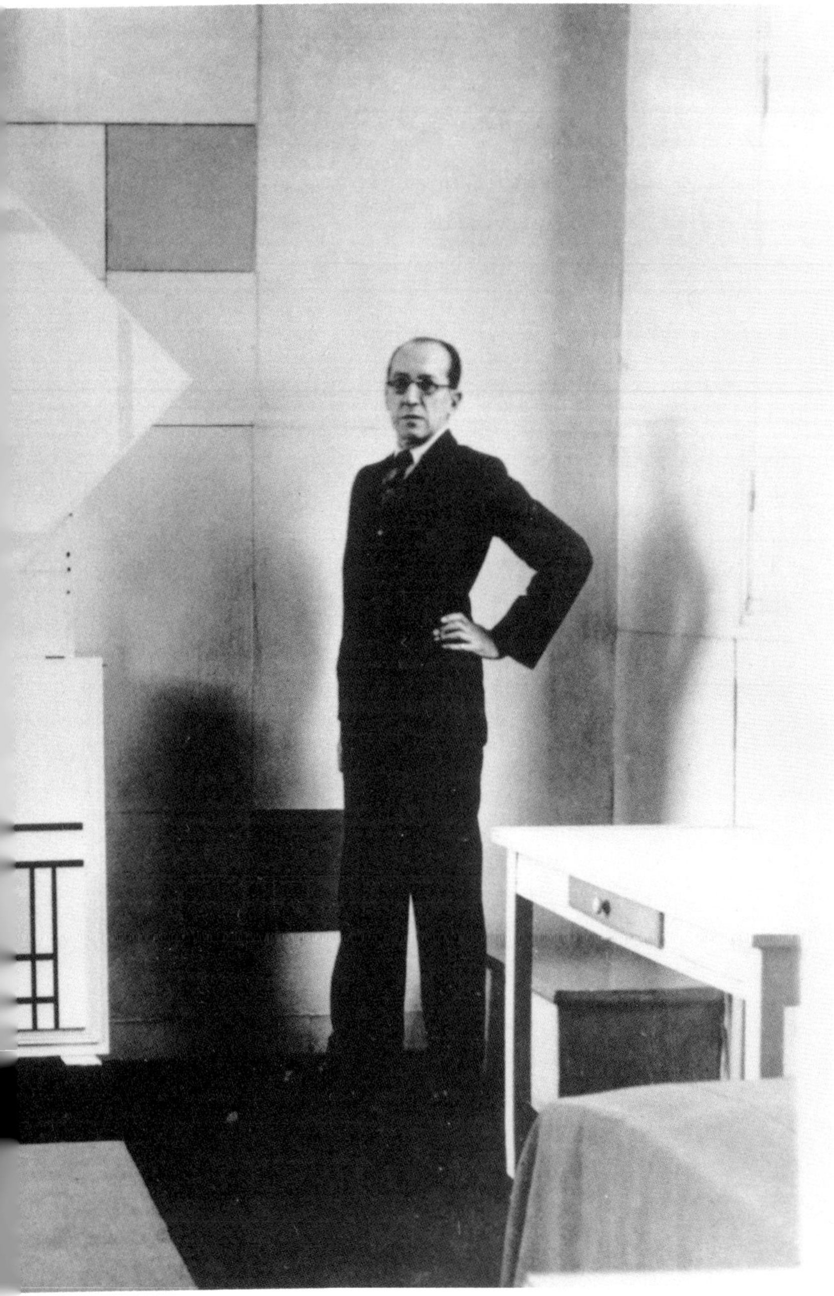

Mondrian spent the last twenty-five years of his life in three of the most politically and culturally important cities of modernism: he was in Paris for the longest period, namely, from the end of 1911 to 1938, albeit with an interruption from 1914 to 1919 caused by World War I. He lived in London from 1938 to 1940. Then he moved to New York, where he died on February 1, 1944, at the age of seventy-one.

In all three metropolises Mondrian got along well; that was not only because he had a talent for languages and was undaunted by expressing himself in writing in the language in question. As a member of the Theosophical Society, → Theosophy he belonged to a group that set great store by its internationality. He also easily established contacts with other people. Finally, he had been a famous avant-gardist since the 1920s. Mondrian's fame was, of course, based on his paintings. But his studios were also legendary places that were extraordinarily inspiring, especially for younger artists. Willem de Kooning (1904–1997) was one of them. The compatriot and exponent of Abstract Expressionism supposedly said of a visit to the New York studio that it was like moving around in one of Mondrian's paintings.[15]

One could not describe the studios better. Not only did he work there in an intense and concentrated way, he also reflected just as long about the paintings he was making in them.

Mondrian's studios are places for thinking that find a counterpart in his paintings.

The studios in all three cities were finished the same: white walls; simple furniture, usually painted white; colorful cardboard boxes along the walls, whose position was repeatedly changed to test out new color effects. And the paintings on which he was working, often several at once. And then there was the gramophone.→Jazz

Q→ Israël Querido

Together with his fellow painters Jan Sluyters and Kees Spoor, Mondrian rented rooms in the Stedelijk Museum in Amsterdam in early January 1909 to organize an exhibition that was on view until January 29 and was seen by 3,000 visitors.

Mondrian presumably wanted to take stock of his art up to that point; he had broken with traditional landscape painting. Thanks to his study of Impressionism, with the work of Vincent van Gogh, and with the Symbolist Luminism of Jan Toroop, his brushwork had become freer, and his palette had brightened enormously. He had also grappled intensely with theosophy →Theosophy and was seeking a way to design his paintings to convey a spiritual dimension.

Mondrian's setup for the exhibition, to the extent it can be reconstructed, was presumably based on the idea of a triptych:[16] the most recent painting was shown in the center of a group, usually of three works. That was not only what confused the visitors: the apparent explosion of colors was too much of a good thing for many. One critic considered the works an expression of decadence and mental illness. Mondrian's *Mill in Sunlight* (1908) →p. 83 in particular triggered discussions.

The naturalist writer Israël Querido (1872–1932), who was famous in the Netherlands at the time, saw the matter differently. His enthusiastic, expressive description *The Mill* conveys an impression of the emotions that this painting triggered:

"I have never seen such murderous colors. The flames are cooking. The contours of the mill bleed in red and also scorching yellow. The blood streams. Golden yellow, India yellow, and cadmium yellow light with radiant vermilion and orange falls like a rain of colors from the scorched sky. . . . Feel along with this flood, with this fulminant glow, with heat blazing into the distance, with these crackling flames of fire of the infernally gnawing embers of the day in the open space of the sun."[17]

Q *Mill; Mill in Sunlight*
[Mill in Sunlight: The Winkel Mill] 1908
Oil on canvas 114.8 × 87 cm
Kunstmuseum Den Haag

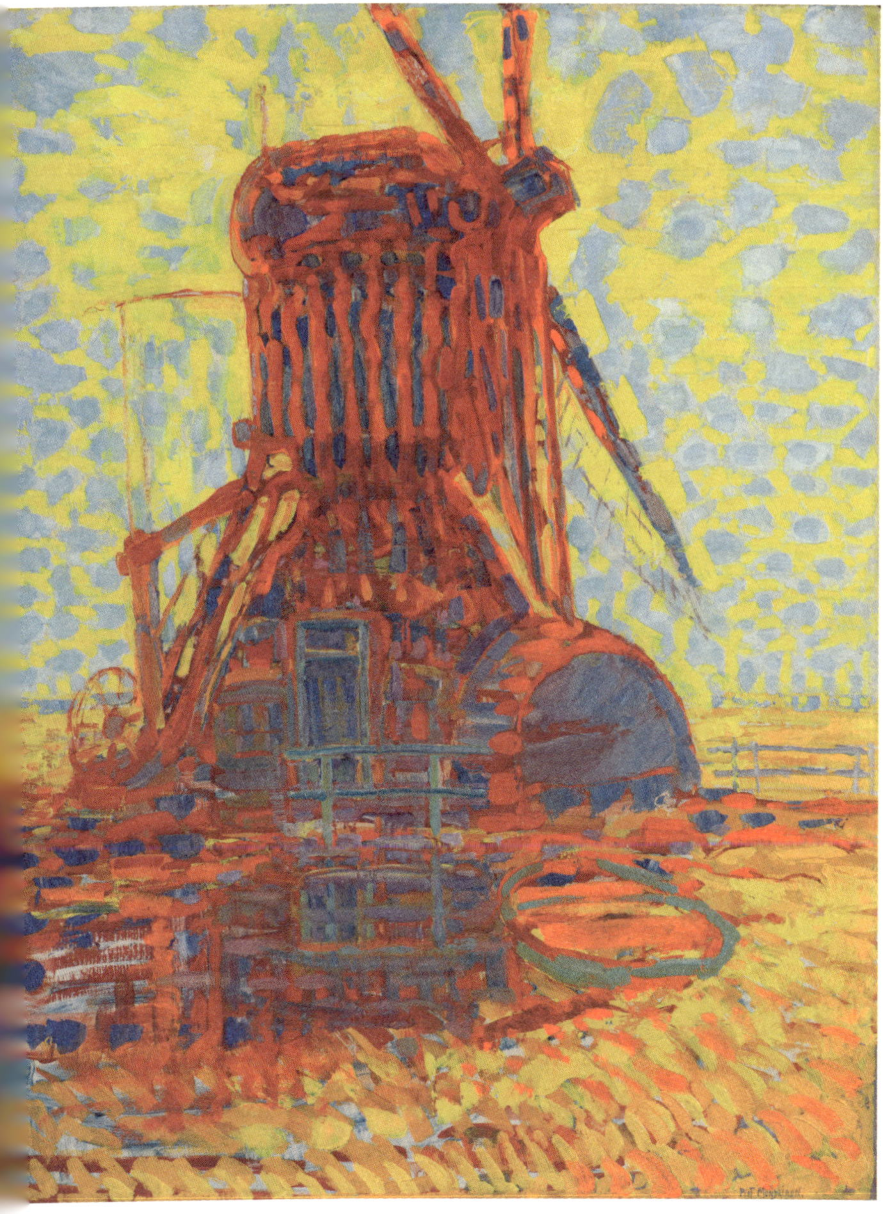

R → Rhythm

One of the most important terms that Mondrian used again and again to explain his intentions is "rhythm."[18] It is not easy to understand what he meant by it. When we speak of a rhythm in art, we might think of the rows of poplars reflected in water that Claude Monet painted: lining up the same forms results in a regularity and hence a visual rhythm.

Mondrian also recreated pictures of rows of trees that depict the proportion of recurring forms.→Gein What distinguished him from other painters, however, is that he presumably, especially in his later paintings, truly wanted to make the idea of a musical rhythm visible.

Mondrian was enthusiastic about jazz.→Jazz Jazz is based on relatively regularly beats, out of which a rhythm develops that calls this regularity into question but nevertheless returns to it over and over. The crucial term here is syncope, a form that deviates from the regular beats, producing the musical tension. That is what "gets into our legs" when listening to jazz or other musical forms evolved from jazz: music for dancing.

Perhaps the dance-mad Mondrian →Foxtrot had something similar in mind with his paintings of "Neoplasticism." →Nieuwe Beelding His compositions, which are never symmetrical, reveal a tension-filled balance that makes a dynamic—

or, better, a rhythm—visible in the first place, albeit only after long, intense viewing of the work.

R A painting with a particularly pronounced rhythm?
No. VI / Composition No. II 1920
Oil on canvas 99.7 × 100.3 cm
Tate Modern, London

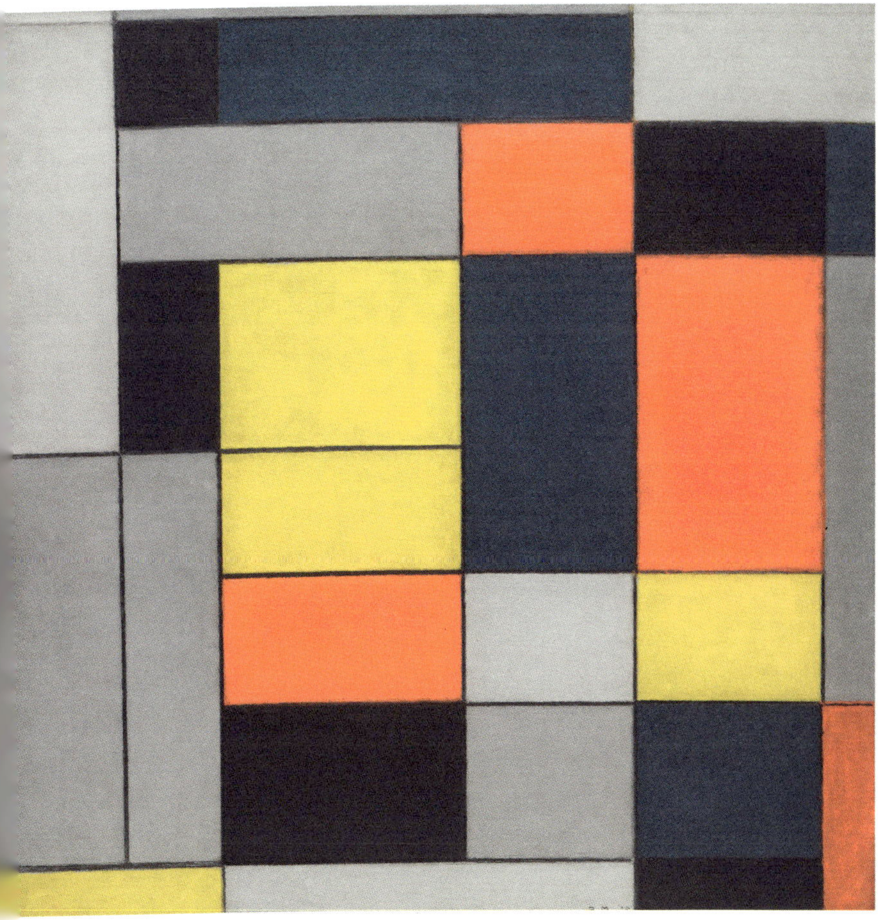

s → De Stijl

After the old values of Europe had vanished in the battles of matériel of World War I, many artists were attempting a radically new cultural beginning. In the Netherlands, which was then neutral, a loose group of like-minded avant-gardists formed, and their publication was the journal *De Stijl* (Style). The founding members included Piet Mondrian, the painter and sculptor Georges Vantongerloo,[→Vantongerloo] and the painter and art theorist Theo van Doesburg, who edited the journal. The first issue appeared in October 1917. Mondrian published the "De Nieuwe Beelding in de Schilderkunst" (Neoplasticism in Painting) in it, and other articles on what would later become famous as Neoplasticism. Mondrian formulated the ambition of this group of artists to destroy traditions in order to redesign all aspects of life based on the essential elements of art it advocated (right angle, black, white, and the primary colors).

That is the reason why, when we think of De Stijl, we first think primarily of design and architecture, such as the famous chair by Gerrit Rietveld (member of the group from 1918) or the architectural designs of the likes of Cornelis van Eesteren (member from 1922), which broke down traditional concepts of space and depicted it as a space-time continuum.

As always when many individualists get together, there were soon differences of opinion: Mondrian, for example, left the group in 1923.

It must remain an open question whether his rejection of Van Doesburg's introduction of diagonal lines was the sole reason. Many members had presumably had a problem with the intuitive element in his compositions. De Stijl meant a great deal of exact geometry, but Mondrian allowed that only to a very limited extent when constructing his compositions. → Intuition and Precision

S Cover of the first issue of the journal *De Stijl* 1917
Original design by Vilmos Huszár

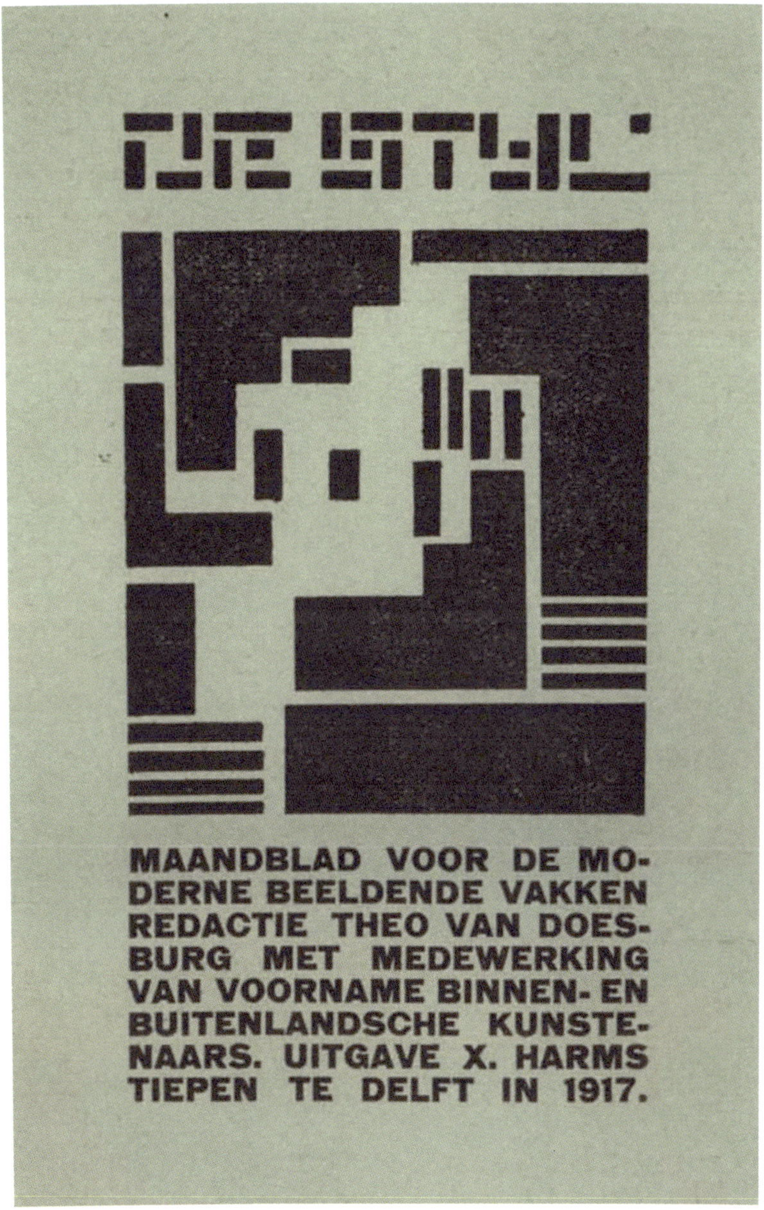

T→ Theosophy

Mondrian's relationship to theosophy was complicated. It is certain that he belonged to the Theosophical Society from 1909 onward, but he did not always get along with its members. It is also certain that the initial space for his intense study of theosophy came from Rudolf Steiner (1861–1925), the founder of anthroposophy. Mondrian had presumably heard Steiner lecture on theosophy in March 1908 in Amsterdam; a copy of the minutes in Dutch of Steiner's discussions, which he annotated, was in his possession until he died. Mondrian's conviction that in his abstract works → Abstraction he could get as close as possible to an absolute, essential truth was probably influenced by theosophical ideas. In principle, theosophy is founded as "divine wisdom" on the pantheistic idea of a mystical, spiritual world related to God, which can be experienced thanks to the ability of intuitive, mystical vision.

Mondrian's abstract paintings are the result of a long process of work in the tension between intuition and precision → Intuition and Precision and of intense observation of his own. The practice of concentrated meditation must ideally be appropriated by all who view his paintings. This opens up access to the absolute, and one might also say, to the divine. That was, perhaps, Mondrian's theosophic vision.

It is interesting that in 1921 Mondrian sent a copy of his text *Le Néo-Plasticisme* to Rudolf Steiner

T Mystical vision?
Self-Portrait (Self-Portrait Eyes) 1908
Charcoal on paper, 30 × 25.5 cm
Kunstmuseum Den Haag

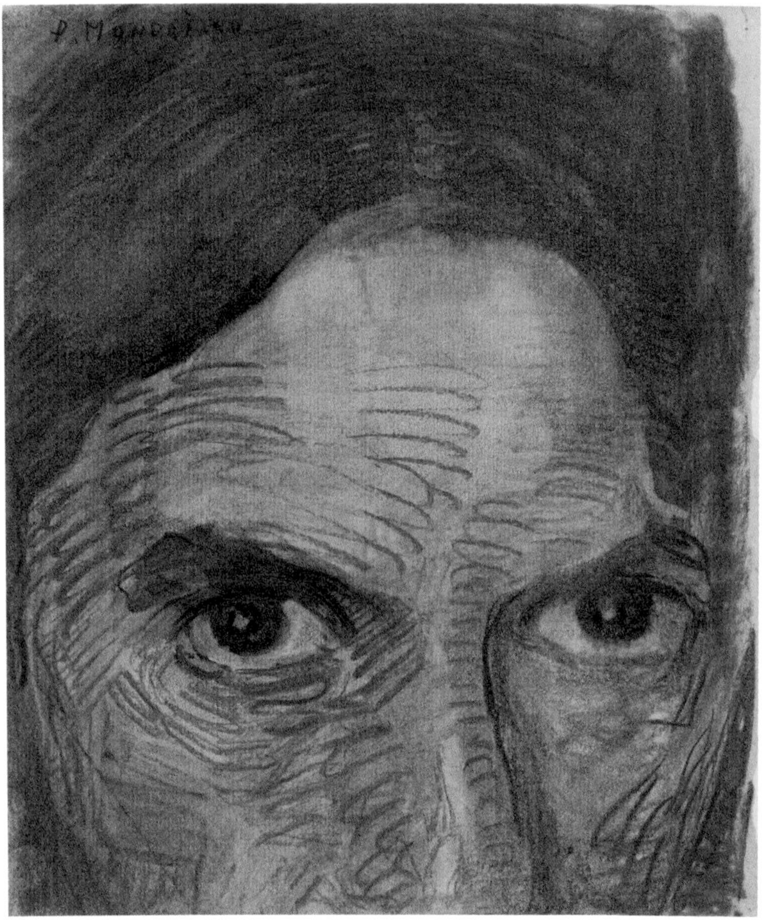

asking for his opinion. He was convinced that in the future Neoplasticism would be the art of the true anthroposophists and theosophists because it created harmony by means of the equal weight of both extremes: the universal and the individual. Art was said to be the visual expression of the evolution of life: the evolution of the spirit and following, from that, of matter. Unfortunately, Rudolf Steiner did not respond.[19]

U →

Jan Braet von Uberfeldt

Jan Braet von Uberfeldt (1807–1894) was a Dutch painter who has fallen into obscurity today. His few known works are somewhat anemic portraits of Dutch high society in the style of the likes of Franz Xaver Winterhalter, sentimental, late Nazarene biblical scenes, and lithographed illustrations of Dutch traditional costume—not a great artist, but one who could paint and render exactly. He also wrote a handbook on drawing from nature for use in elementary schools. Mondrian, whose first career was teaching drawing, visited him frequently around 1890.

Braet von Uberfeldt, whom time and the evolution of art passed by, lived with his young wife and a goat in Doetinchem, a good half-hour by train from Winterswijk, where the Mondrian family lived. He was perhaps the first professional artist whom Mondrian met. He visited him frequently and was fascinated by his collection of all sorts of painted reproductions, *vedute*, and newspaper illustrations that Von Uberfeldt had put together. Mondrian's knowledge of art history probably derived from that and perhaps also a sense of the dilemma in which many nineteenth-century artists in the Netherlands (but not just there) believed they were stuck, namely, being completely dependent on the art of earlier periods. In the Netherlands it was the so-called Golden Age in the seventeenth century. The painters of that time were still setting the standards for the later nineteenth century. Mondrian also painted in this style, as his *Still Life with Dead Hare* of 1891 shows. It looks like an imitation of a painting by Jan Weenix that he had seen either in the Rijksmuseum in Amsterdam or as in illustration at the home of Braet von Uberfeldt.

U *Dead Hare* 1891
Oil on canvas 80 × 51 cm
Kunstmuseum Den Haag

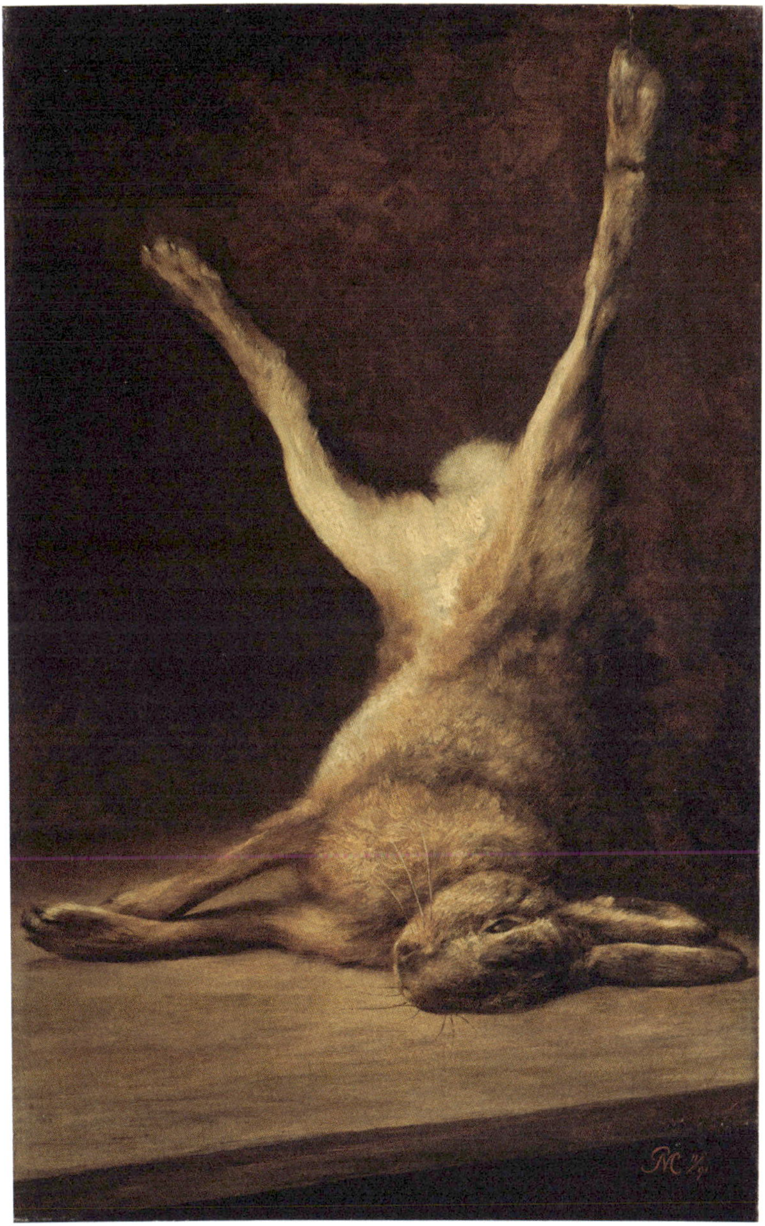

V → Georges Vantongerloo

The Belgian artist Georges Vantongerloo (1886–1965) serves here as a representative of many artists who were powerfully influenced by Piet Mondrian, who was more than ten years older, but who found their own path to develop further. Vantongerloo was wounded in the German invasion of Belgium in 1914 and then fled to the Netherlands, where he played an important role in the establishment of the artists' group De Stijl.→De Stijl Later, the two men became increasingly estranged, though Mondrian did become a member of the artists' group Abstraction-Création, which Vantongerloo initiated in 1931.

In "De Realiseering van het Neo-Plasticisme in verre toekomst en in de huidige Architectuur" (The Realization of Neo-Plasticism in the Distant Future and in Architecture Today), an essay published in the journal *De Stijl* in 1922, Mondrian succinctly assessed the role of his colleague: "Once realized in painting, the Neoplastic concept was manifested in sculpture (Vantongerloo's prismatic compositions)."[20] He was alluding to the abstract, geometric for which Vantongerloo is primarily famous today. In contrast to Piet Mondrian, who only accepted the rectangle in his paintings, Vantongerloo also introduced the circle, for example, into his abstractions. The big difference between the two artists' concepts of art was probably Vantongerloo's idea that art functioned based on universal mathematical laws inherent in it that one had to seek and understand. Mondrian seems to have preferred

V Florence Henri, Visitors in Piet Mondrians studio, from left to right Rosie Ney, Georges Vantongerloo, Lancelot Ney, Tine Vantongerloo, Michel Seuphor and Piet Mondriaan

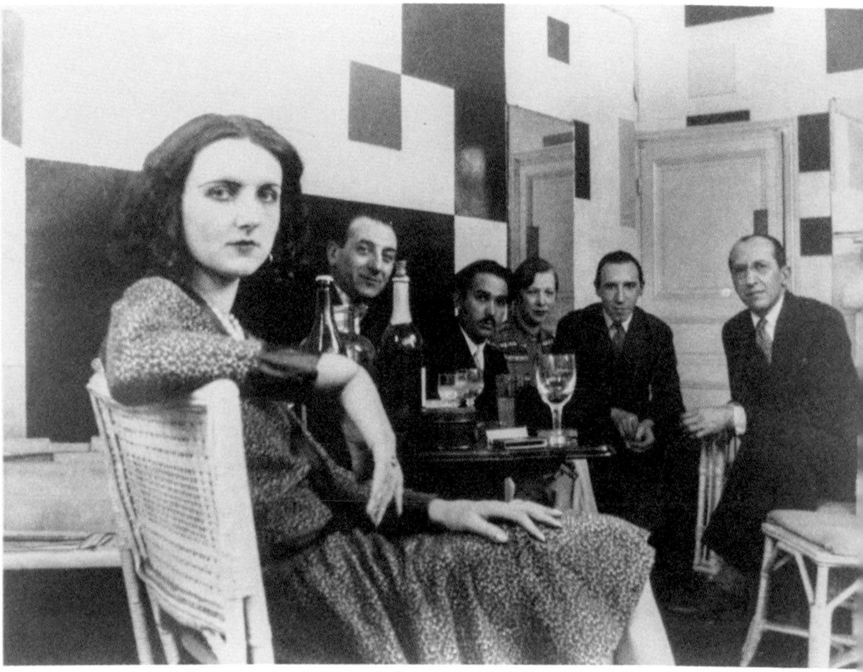

to rely on his artistic intuition, which in the end cannot be justified rationally.

W → Windmills

The windmill is—along with tulips, cheese, and wooden clogs—a symbol of the Netherlands, but perhaps especially of Holland,[→Holland] that is to say, the provinces of Noord-Holland and Zuid-Holland. Like church spires, windmills are orientation points that can be seen from afar in this flat landscape with an open sky. The rotating sails symbolize eternal movement and point to the hard work of their operators: mills were used not only to grind grains but also to drain the polders created by land reclamation. They have been painted over and over since the seventeenth century.

They were also a popular motif for Mondrian. Just as he painted the farm in Duivendrecht [→Duivendrecht] and drew the mill in Blaricum in several versions, even as late as 1917, after he had really abandoned representationalism in his art. It is not entirely clear whether these were commissioned works; in any case, the form of the windmill appears abstracted almost into a planar symbol. That is especially clear in the version in which the mill is no longer seen as a three-dimensional volume but essentially only its shadow backlit by the moon. As was already the case with the farm in Duivendrecht, Mondrian appears to have been experimenting here with how far abstraction could go without abandoning representationalism.

W *Windmill in the Evening* 1917
Oil on canvas 103 × 86 cm
Kunstmuseum Den Haag

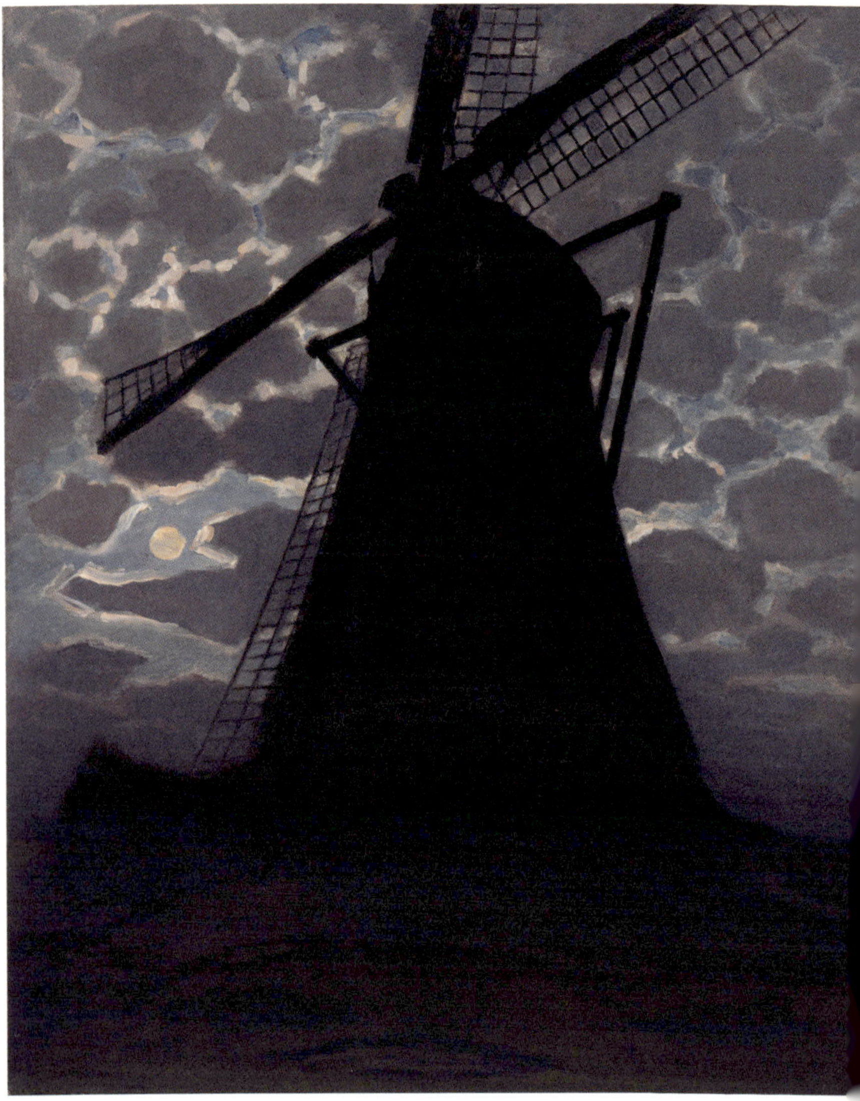

x → Xcéron

X Study for *Composition with Red, Yellow, and Blue* 1930
Gouache on cardboard 28.6 × 22.9 cm
Triton Collection Foundation

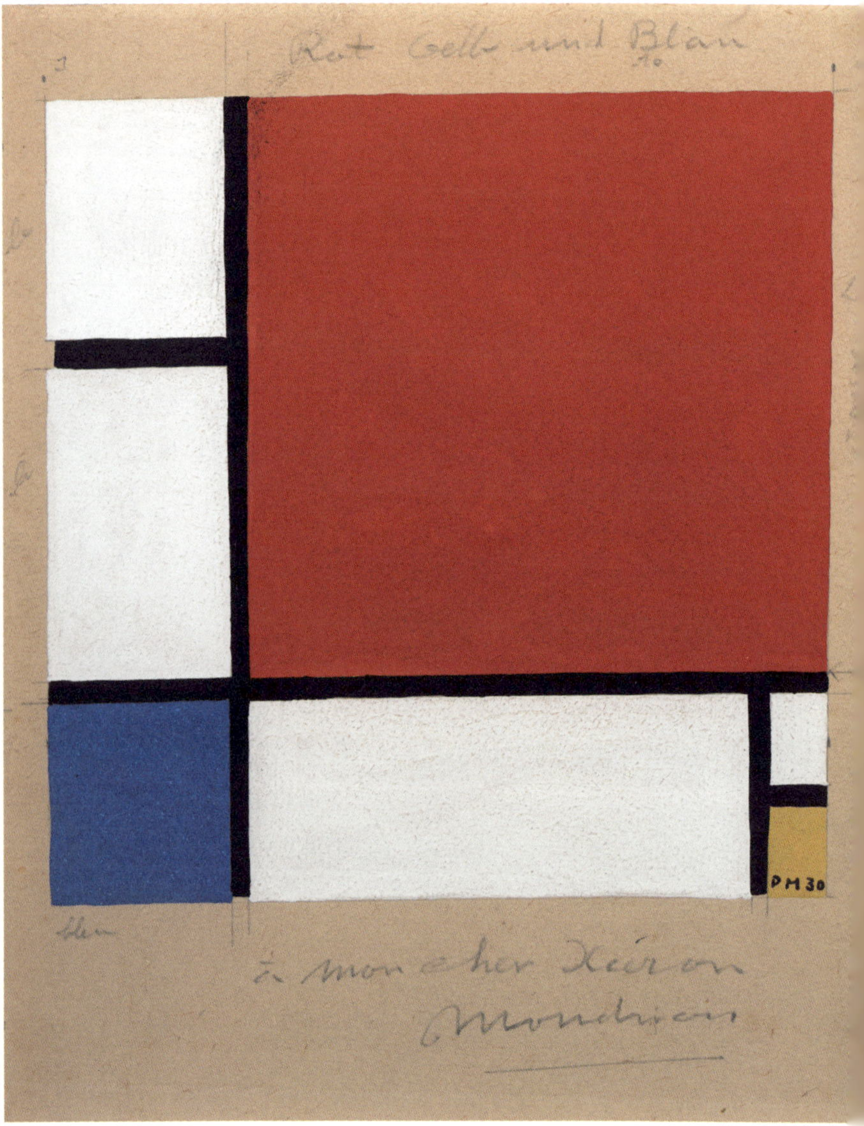

Jean Xcéron (1890–1967) was a painter and art critic. He was a great admirer of Piet Mondrian's art. In 1929, he reported very positively about him in the *Chicago Tribune*. Xcéron visited Mondrian in his studio and received a precious gift—with a dedication and signature—namely, one of the few surviving gouache studies for a painting.→p.108 The finished painting is now owned by a Japanese bank. Mondrian had probably intended to give the sheet to a German collection, which is why he labeled it on top in German "Rot Gelb und Blau" (Red, Yellow, and Blue).

In 1938, Mondrian wrote from London to Xcéron, the architect Frederick Kiesler, and the artist Harry Holtzman, who would later become Mondrian's heir, asking to be invited to come to the United States. Nothing came of it; Mondrian did not emigrate to New York until 1940, after the live-in studio he had moved into as a guest of the painter Ben Nicholson had been damaged in an aerial bombardment.

Y → YSL

The fashion designer Yves Saint Laurent was inspired by his reading of Michel Seuphor's biography of Mondrian, published in 1956, to create a series of dress designs, which he marketed in the summer of 1965. Saint Laurent had apparently never seen a Mondrian painting in the original; later, however, he and his partner, Pierre Bergé, owned four works by the painter, including *Composition with Blue, Red, Yellow, and Black*, a vertical-format work from 1922 (catalogue raisonné B142).

None of the designs appear to have been based directly on a Mondrian painting. They are free designs that adopted Mondrian's principles of "Neoplasticism": [→ Nieuwe Beelding] white as the basic color, black lines at right angles as well as blue, red, and yellow, and straight lines. The enthusiastic fashion press—not Saint Laurent himself—coined the term "Mondrian dress." The Mondrian dresses marked a milestone in art merchandising. Indeed, perhaps modern museum shops would look quite different today without these ideas.

This raises the questions: Should one be allowed to do this sort of thing with an artist? Doesn't this devalue the work? For Mondrian, Neoplasticism, whose principles he had formulated in the journal *De Stijl*, [→ De Stijl] applied to all spheres of life, including fashion. Certainly, one cannot truly copy a painting by Mondrian and reproduce it. The aura of the original is too present for all who seriously engage with it. What is crucial is that Yves Saint Laurent was inspired by Mondrian's ideas and then developed them freely. By doing, he was surely working quite precisely in the spirit of the artist.

Y Yves Saint Laurent cocktail dress
Homage to Piet Mondrian Paris 1965

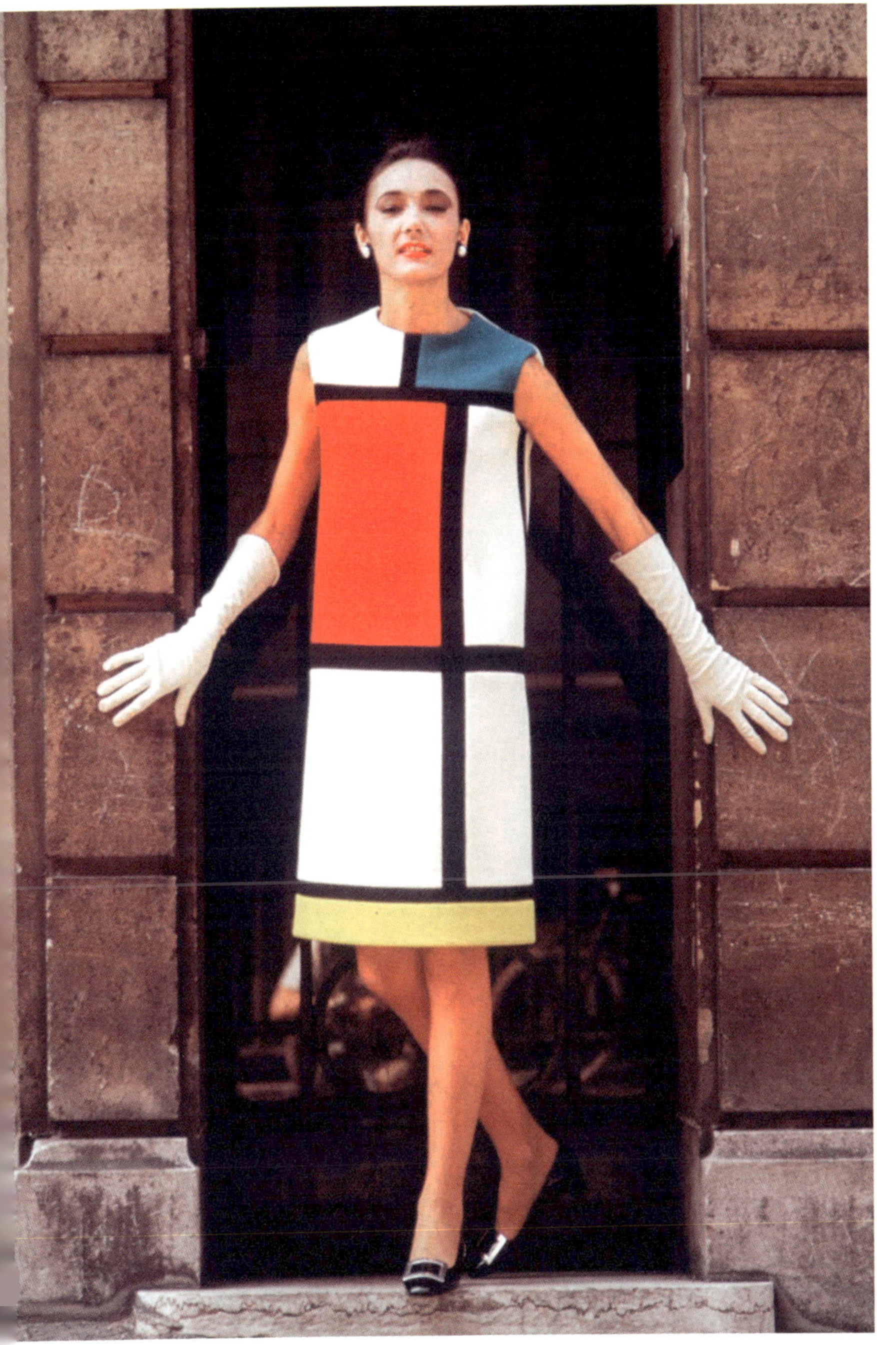

z→ Agathe Zethraeus

Agathe (aka Agatha) Zethraeus (1872–1966) was a Dutch painter. Mondrian gave her drawing lessons for a time. Around 1907 she and Mondrian became a couple. In contrast to his numerous other affairs, this bond was probably quite serious. For a time, Zethraeus was even convinced that their engagement was imminent, but Mondrian ended the relationship in 1908. Nevertheless, the two remained in contact. When Mondrian died on February 1, 1944, of a lung ailment for which he had been treated only too late, an unanswered letter from his friend was found with his correspondence.

Zethraeus was probably not a bad painter, but she never left the traditional paths of the Hague school of painters, which Mondrian had also taken for a long time. She is known for landscapes and *vedute* influenced by Impressionism. Her work did not share the audacity that characterized Mondrian's artistic evolution.

Mondrian's powerful depiction of a girl from 1908 is thought to be an idealized portrait of Agathe and can be interpreted as evidence of the intensity of their relationship. But perhaps the painting is rather the illustration of a color situation described by Johann Wolfgang von Goethe in chapter 5 of his *Farbenlehre* (Theory of Color, 1810): one evening at dusk a girl with a white face and a red bodice enters an inn; after she had left, Goethe saw a black face on the white wall and instead of red a sea green.[21]

Mondrian admired Goethe and his *Farbenlehre*. Inspired by Goethe, he studied perception and the effect of color all his life.

Z *Portrait of a Girl* 1908
Oil on canvas on wood 49 × 41.5 cm
Kunstmuseum Den Haag

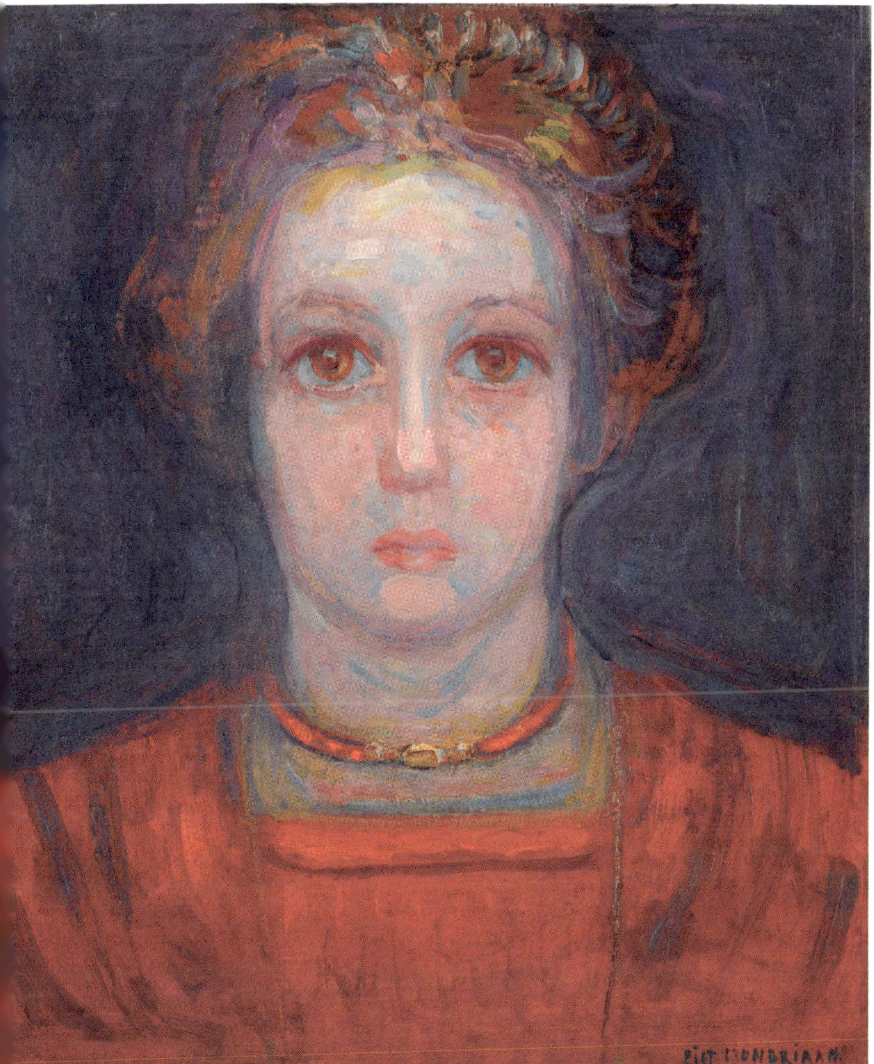

Endnotes

1 Piet Mondrian to Hendricus Peter Bremmer, January 29, 1914, in *Mondrian and Cubism*, ed. Hans Janssen, exh. cat. Gemeentemuseum, The Hague (London, 2015), pp. 54–55, esp. p. 54.

2 On Mondrian's "Cubism," see Hans Janssen, ed., *Mondrian and Cubism* (see note 1).

3 This interpretation follows the ideas of Robert Welsh, published in 1971. See Hans Janssen, *Piet Mondrian: Vom Abbild zum Bild* (The Hague, 2008), pp. 153–57. On the concept of "evolution" in Mondrian, see Hans Janssen, "A Modern Evolution," in *Mondrian & De Stijl*, exh. cat. Museo Reina Sofia (Madrid, 2020), pp. 42–44.

4 Hans Janssen, *Piet Mondriaan: Een nieuwe Kunst voor en ongekend leven; Een Biografie* (Amsterdam, 2016), p. 395.

5 Ibid., p. 63.

6 See the Piet Mondrian Conservation Project, www.fondationbeyeler.ch/pietmondrianconservationproject.

7 On Mondrian's relationship to jazz, see, for example, Katjuscha Otte, "All that Jazz: Victory Boogie Woogie," in *Piet Mondrian: The Studios*, ed. Cees de Jong (London, 2015), pp. 190–97.

8 Marek Wieczorek, "Rhythms of Life: The Reception of Mondrian's *Victory Boogie Woogie*," in *Inside Out: Victory Boogie Woogie: A Material History of Mondrian's Masterpiece*, ed. Maarten van Bommel et al. (Amsterdam, 2011), pp. 245–79, esp. p. 251.

9 Mary Gabriel, *Ninth Street Women* (New York, 2018), pp. 81–82.

10 Lee Krasner mentioned this episode twice in interviews with Dorothy Seckler. The version of April 11, 1968, is here: Archives of American Art, transcript, www.aaa.si.edu/collections/interviews/oral-history-interview-lee-krasner-12507#transcript.

11 Piet Mondrian, *Toward the True Vision of Reality* (New York, 1942), reprinted in Mondrian, *The Complete Writings*, ed. Louis Veen (Leiden, 2017), pp. 490–94, esp. p. 491.

12 See Janssen 2016 (see note 4), p. 216.

13 On this, see Marek Wieczorek, "The Gradual Evolution of Mondrian's Neoplasticism," in Janssen 2020 (see note 3), pp. 92–95. Perhaps Mondrian's most accessible text on Neoplasticism and its importance in the design of modern life is "Neo-Plasticisme: De Woning, De Straat, De Stad," *Internationale revue i10* (1927). Reprinted in Veen 2017 (see note 11), pp. 269–75. English translation in de Jong 2015 (see note 7), pp. 140–53.

14 Marek Wieczorek pointed this out to me.

15 De Kooning's remark was passed on by Harry Holtzman. Quoted in Ingelies Vermeulen, "'Like Walking Around in One of Mondrian's Paintings': Mondrian's Last Studios in New York," in de Jong 2015 (see note 7), pp. 172–81, esp. p. 179.

16 See Hans Janssen, "A Unique Personal Quest," in Janssen 2020 (see note 3), pp. 11–21, esp. pp. 19–21.

17 Quoted in Janssen 2020 (see note 3), pp. 122–24.

18 See Caro Verbeek, "Looking to Piet's Beat: Mondrian's Inaudible Rhythms," in *Mondrian Evolution*, exh. cat. Fondation Beyeler Riehen/Basel; Kunstsammlung Nordrhein-Westfalen Düsseldorf (Berlin, 2022), pp. 178–83.

19 On Mondrian and Steiner, see Jacqueline van Paaschen, *Mondriaan en Steiner: Wegen naar Nieuwe Beelding* (The Hague, 1917). Reproduction of Mondrian's letter to Steiner, p. 130. Reproduction of Mondrian's annotated copy of Steiner's lectures, pp. 149–81.

20 See Veen 2017 (see note 11), p. 216: "Gerealiseerd in de Schilderkunst, heeft het Neo-Plastisch begrip zich ook in Beeldhouwkunst uitgesproken (prisma-composities van G. Vantongerloo)." English translation in Piet Mondrian, "The Realization of Neoplasticism in the Distant Future and in Architecture Today," trans. Hans L. C. Jaffé, in *De Stijl* (New York, 1986), pp. 164–71, esp. p. 167.

21 See Janssen 2020 (see note 3), p. 117.

Credits

Biography

Pieter Cornelis Mondriaan (later stylized Piet Mondrian) was born on March 7, 1872, in Amersfoort, the Netherlands. After training to be a drawing teacher and studying art in Amsterdam, he worked as an art teacher, scientific draftsman, and portraitist. Setting out from traditional landscape painting, he developed an expressive painting style of strong colors. In 1912, he moved to Paris. His encounter with Cubism led to a series of nonrepresentational paintings in subdued colors. Mondrian spent World War I in the Netherlands and continued to work on forms of abstraction (representational and nonrepresentational). He was a founding member of the De Stjil movement. After returning to Paris in 1919, Mondrian concentrated on abstract painting consisting of rectangles, black lines, white, and the primary colors yellow, red, and blue. After an interim stop in London, Mondrian emigrated to New York in 1940. There, he began to experiment with colorful lines in his paintings. He died in New York on February 1, 1944.

Acknowledgments and Dedication

Thanks to Markus Gross, Richard Hagemann, Doede Hardeman, Hans Janssen†, Sam Keller, Charlotte Sarrazin, Friederike Steckling, Benno Tempel, Caro Verbeek, Nicola von Velsen, and Marek Wieczorek.

For Annina, Leonard, and Andreas

Colophon

The concept of the A-Z series is based on an idea by Ulf Küster.

Copyediting Aaron Bogart
Translations Steven Lindberg
Graphic design Torsten Köchlin, Joana Katte
Typeface Scto Grotesk A
Production Thomas Lemaître
Reproductions DLG, Paris
Paper Munken Lynx, 150 g/m²
Printing DZS GRAFIK, d. o. o., Ljubljana

Published by
Hatje Cantz Verlag GmbH
Mommsenstraße 27
10629 Berlin
www.hatjecantz.com

A Ganske Publishing Group Company

ISBN 978-3-7757-5248-0 (English edition)
ISBN 978-3-7757-5247-3 (German edition)

Printed in Slovenia

Cover illustration
Staff of Gemeentemuseum The Hague
in Mondrian dresses by Yves Saint Laurent,
January 1966. photo: Eric Koch/Anefo

Frontispiece
Piet Mondrian, May 12, 1899